Papers presented at the
First Australian Consultation

Towards a Theology of Youth Ministry

Ridley College, Melbourne

1998

Published July 1999

By Aquila Press
PO Box A287, Sydney South, NSW 1235

© S. Hale and S. Bazzana (eds) June 1999

Apart from any fair dealing for the purposes of private study, research, criticism or review as permitted under the Copyright Act, no part of this publication may be reproduced by any process without written permission from the publishers.

The Scripture quotations contained herein are from the New Revised Standard Version Bible copyright 1989 by the Division of Christian Education of the National Council of the Churches of Christ in the USA. Used by permission. All rights reserved.

National Library of Australia
ISBN 1 875861 55 6

Cover art by Jo Sterland

Printed in Australia by Alken Press Pty Ltd

Acknowledgment

Our thanks go to the Anglican General Synod for its assistance in enabling this book to be published.

Contents

Acknowledgment		iii
Introduction		vii
1.	Relational theology and its impact on youth ministry *Trevor Hunter*	1
2.	The Trinity, the historical Jesus and youth ministry *Angus McLeay*	19
3.	A theological model of youth ministry *Stephen Hale*	35
4.	Developing persons in the local church *Mark Leach*	47
5.	Youth ministry and the postmodern self *Andrew Stewart*	57
6.	Worship, community and the triune God of Grace *Olivia Moffatt*	71
7.	Youth and the experience of the Holy Spirit *John Gray*	87
8.	A relational theology of youth ministry *Peter Hotchkin*	105
9.	Dying for a reason to live *Brad Lovegrove*	117
10.	You are what you are called: Trinity, self and vocation *Gordon Preece*	133
11.	Discipline, a reflective conversation *Roger Bray*	153
12.	The charismatic leader, change and the institutionalised church *David Rietveld*	165

Introduction

'A Theology of Youth Ministry' has been considered by some people to be a contradiction in terms! However in mid-1996 the Anglican General Synod Youth Commission stepped out and agreed to facilitate what it believes was the first conference of its kind in Australia, the First Australian Consultation Towards a Theology of Youth Ministry.

For a number of years various people had spoken about how youth ministry in Australia had focused on the practical aspects of the ministry and that very few people were thinking about biblical theology as it relates to youth ministry. We were stuck in the 'how to' stage and not really spending much time thinking about 'why' or 'where to next'.

The conference was seen as a step forward, one which would get people thinking about youth ministry in a different way. We were clear that it was not going to be yet another 'how to' conference but something that would really attempt to break new ground and showcase new ideas.

The Youth Commission approached Ridley College and Anglican Youth Ministries, both in the Diocese of Melbourne, to organise the conference, and a small committee was established. It was agreed that we would try to attract papers from younger theologians and youth ministry practitioners to provide input to the conference. The key would be in the new ideas and the academic rigour of the papers to be presented.

Great enthusiasm for the concept was shown and over sixty people attended the conference. They were challenged by the material, and discussion is under way for a second conference to take place in 2000.

This book is a collation of the papers presented at the conference, which we hope will broaden the impact of youth ministry in this country and around the world.

Sue Bazzana and Stephen Hale

CHAPTER ONE

Relational theology and its impact on youth ministry

Trevor Hunter

Youth ministry and theology

What is the theological basis for youth ministry? This seems a fair question to ask at the beginning of a lecture designed to stimulate thought in this area. Many argue that the real concerns of youth focus on the world in which they live, age-related developmental goals and the various facets of their subculture. Some say that the reason the church is having a declining influence on young people is because of its failure to engage this subculture and failure to address itself to those needs. Others argue that only these needs can provide a rationale for youth ministry since the Bible itself is so silent on youth. The end result of this logic is 'youth ministers' who are essentially social or welfare workers, believing that their primary role is to understand the youth culture rather than understand the Christian faith and apply it to that culture.

During this lecture I hope to impress upon you that the failure to engage in effective and life shaping youth ministry is not so much due to a failure to take youth culture seriously as a failure to take the Bible sufficiently seriously.[1] Put it another way. There are two imperatives for effective youth ministry I believe. The first is to take the world in which young people live seriously, yet even more importantly we must take seriously God's word to them in the Bible.

Even for evangelical Christians the central place of the Bible in youth ministry can be under threat and that for obvious reasons. The Bible contains no systematic theology of youth. There is no mention of

---

1. For a fuller discussion on this point see M. Ashton, *Christian Youth Work* (Eastbourne: Kingsway, 1986), 56–66.

teenagers, or youth workers. Adolescents were not regarded as a significant group in the ancient world as they are today. I suspect this is why there has been little written from evangelicals by way of a theological rationale for youth ministry. A plethora of books have been written on 'how to' – few if any on 'why do', which is disappointing given that evangelicals have always been a vanguard in the theological area.

That is not to say there is no information of relevance in the Bible to help us formulate the priority and practice of youth ministry. The issue of an effective rationale for youth ministry cannot be decided by recourse to other disciplines such as sociology or adolescent psychology or even modern educational theory. A decision to work with youth in an evangelical sense cannot be based on the premise that they have special emotional or educational needs or that they are going through a difficult stage in life. Youth Ministry is not derivative, dependant on the primary place of non-theological disciplines. Neither is it synthetic, a conglomeration of those disciplines with a biblical gloss. *Youth ministry derives its rationale from the very nature of biblical theology which at its heart is relational.* Simply put, evangelical youth ministry is drawn from the wellspring of relational theology, which is itself a true expression of biblical theology. What then is the connection between theology and relationship?

I want to answer that question by looking at some general considerations, and then examining the theological contribution to this area by Broughton Knox.

Knowledge and relationship

All too often the Ministry of the Word has been translated into 'the study of God' whereby the object of the ministry is to expand the mind and increase knowledge about God. Theological knowledge for its own sake is bound to go sour and leave a person proud and conceited.[2] As Paul says in 1 Corinthians 8:1, 'Knowledge puffs up, but love builds up'. Surely the proper object of any Christian passion and concern ought to be God himself: his character and purposes and how he has revealed them. Psalm 119 echoes the desire a person can have for God's

---

2. I am here using the analysis put forward by J.I. Packer in his book *Knowing God* (London: Hodder and Stoughton, 1985). His opening chapters on the difference between studying God and knowing God are particularly valuable.

revealed truth: 'teach me your statutes'; 'open my eyes to see the wonderful things in your law'; 'O how I love your law'. But what was the object of such study? Not simply knowledge but *praxis*, how to live a life in conformity to God's will: 'you are good and your ways are good, teach me your decrees'; 'oh that my ways were directed to keep your statutes'; 'teach me O Lord to follow your decrees and I will keep them to the end'. Not simply knowledge but *relationship*, to know God and in the process draw closer to him: 'I have sought your face with all my heart, be gracious to me according to your promise'; 'may your unfailing love be my comfort'; 'let your compassion come to me that I may live'.

So God is not an object that we study. He is the author and ruler of our endeavours to know him. He alone makes such study possible that we might be led into relationship with him. As did the psalmist, we study God in order that he might engage and deal with us so we might better serve him as we come to know him.

Theology and relationship: D.B. Knox

Broughton Knox was principal of Moore Theological College for 26 years and arguably shaped the College as we find it today, despite his resignation from that post in 1985. It is not for me to make an assessment of his wider theological contribution to evangelical thought.[3] However, I believe his contribution in providing a rationale for relational theology and sourcing it within the Godhead itself is critical for our endeavours. Knox produced little by way of books during his principalship and all too brief retirement, though in this particular area we have his thoughts collated and presented in lecture format and later published as *The Everlasting God*.[4]

The tone of the book is set in the opening statement:

---

3. This has already been done in the collection of essays edited by P.T. O'Brien and D.G. Peterson entitled *The God who is Rich in Mercy* (Homebush: Lancer, 1986).
4. D.B. Knox, *The Everlasting God* (Welwyn: Evangelical Press, 1982). Knox made a wide-ranging contribution to theological endeavour, though his primary interest was in the doctrine of God. This forms the substance of these essays. Their uniqueness and enduring value is due mainly to Knox successfully doing what Packer pleads for: showing how the study of God enriches and deepens relationship with God. To that end I believe he is unique among post Reformation theologians, most of whom sadly departed from the intensely relational theology of Calvin and Luther and in the process managed to turn theological endeavour into an arid and stultifying intellectual process.

> The doctrine of God is of the utmost importance, for it controls the whole of life. As a person thinks about God, that is to say as he thinks about ultimate reality, so his standards of behaviour, values and relations with other people are determined.[5]

For Knox there could be nothing more foundational or indeed critical for Christian reflection than the doctrine of God. From this everything else flowed: the authority of Scripture – God's self revelation; the true nature of Christian worship – how God is to be honoured; the nature of faith – how God is to be received; predestination and perseverance – the sovereignty and grace of God.[6]

There are five loci of Knox's theology that are axiomatic for the development of a relational theology. These will help us to see why relational theology is a true expression of biblical theology.

Concerning the Word

The very existence of revelation predicates personhood argues Knox, for if God exists and is at all personal then revelation will follow. Persons are self-authenticating. When you are addressed by them then you need no other proof of their existence. Thus the Word of God is self-authenticating, for it is a personal word addressed by God to an individual and therefore heard by that person. The foundation for the existence of God and his character is found in that he speaks person-to-person.

Concerning the Trinity

Moving on from his theology of the Word, itself relationally based, we turn to his doctrine of the Trinity which is at its core relational. It is fair to say that Knox, in advocating the primacy of the Trinity[7], is not arguing for something new but reiterating orthodox theology as old as

---

5. Knox, 11. Robert Banks highlights this passage in his appreciation of Knox's theology, commenting that the doctrine of God was his focal concern and the driving force behind a lifetime of theological reflection. See R. Banks, 'The Theology of D.B. Knox', *The God Who is Rich in Mercy*, eds. O'Brien and Peterson, (Homebush: Lancer, 1986), 377–399.
6. Some have argued that Knox's theology lacked a Christocentric dimension. However his argument that all of reformed theology itself had come about as a result of a Christological revolution, meant that, for him at least, all of his theological endeavours were possible only in and through Christ – so Colossians 3:1. However it may also have been that he was reacting against Barth's Christological overemphasis.
7. Knox, 49. The doctrine of the Trinity is the foundation of the Christian religion. Unless this doctrine is held firmly and truly it is not possible to be a Christian.

biblical revelation itself, as formulated in the Athanasian creed. What I think is new is the grounding of that doctrine in a relational framework. As Knox says:

> The doctrine of the Trinity is the glory of the Christian religion. It tells us that ultimate reality is personal relationship. God is ultimate reality ... yet God is not a single monad or impersonal absolute, but God is relationship. He is Father, Son and Holy Spirit.[8]

Therefore relationships ultimately exist in the very heart of reality, for they are present in the very Personhood of God. The characteristic of true relationship is other-person-centred, for that is how we see the relationship between Father, Son and Spirit (John 3:35, 5:20, 8:29, 14:31, 16:13–14). Likewise the relationship is one of intimacy, so close that the will of the Trinity is unified in purpose and action. After moving through the Old and New Testament evidences for the Trinity, Knox brings us to personhood within the Godhead. Since we have a God who reveals himself, by definition God is personal, but personality cannot exist in monad, that is complete singularity of being. Personality requires relationship. If God is spoken of as just or righteous or loving or holy or faithful then these are not things about his character that appeared at creation but are things that have been eternally so. Yet these are personal and relational values rooted in the character of God, that is they express and reflect they way Persons within the Trinity relate to each other. As Knox says:

> This doctrine sheds light on our understanding of human life. From it we realise that personal relationship is of the essence of reality and we also learn something of the true quality of relationship.[9]

Concerning humanity

The Doctrine of the Trinity also enables us to understand what is meant when it is said that God created humankind in his own image. God has created us for relationship, for he is relational.[10]

I believe that for Knox *imagio dei* is not simply moral or functional or even epistemological but is primarily relational. Simply put, our created nature in the image of God is relational. Those characteristics that

---

8. Knox, 51.
9. Knox, 64.
10. Knox, 66.

enable humanity to be relational were not lost at the fall. Sin has made relationships self-serving, lacking the love, kindness, faithfulness and purity that mark divine relationships. When we are deprived of relationships we experience loneliness – a terrible ache that reminds us we were never created to be alone. Augustine's comment in the Confessions, 'you have made us for yourself and our hearts are restless till they find their rest in you', would resonate with Knox at this point.

Concerning language

The problem of religious language is dealt with by relational theology. Human relationships reflect the image of the Trinity. It follows therefore that language reflecting human relationships is suitable to describe the Godhead's relationships within himself and with humanity. Our language is an adequate vehicle to describe God himself. Religious language, 'God Speak', is neither agnostic (so Wittgenstein) nor analogical (so Aquinas) but rather univocal (so Calvin). We can really describe and relate to God through human language. Against the modern proponents of theory or post structuralism we affirm language as a vehicle of truth and knowledge, for it is relationally based and originates in our God who is relational.

Concerning the church

Knox had been at the forefront in the resurgence of interest in the relational core of theology, as witnessed in his final main theological focus, that of the church. Here he argues that the real nature of church is the gathering of believers in one another's presence, having come specifically for that purpose. The gathering is not simply a consequence of our relationship with Christ, but a consequence of our relationship with each other. Fellowship only takes place according to Knox when:

> We can look at each other, face to face. For fellowship consists of a word spoken and responded to, in the context of receiving and appreciating each other.[11]

It is this thoroughgoing relational theology that I think we need to capture to develop an effective theological framework for youth ministry. I want now to consider some applications of relational theology to youth ministry and then draw a conclusion.

---

11. D.B. Knox, 'The Church and the Denominations', *RTR* 23 (1964), 48.

Relational Theology: Directives for Youth Ministry

Faith

I cannot hope to do justice to the biblical teaching on faith in the space of one part of a lecture. It may be sufficient to remind you that *pistis*, the Greek term for faith, is hardly found in isolated noun form in the Gospels, whereas the verbal form *pisteuo*, coupled with a range of prepositions, figures prominently.[12] It is the believing **into** that is the central issue. The **what** or more properly **who** one is believing is the critical usage in the Gospels. So John 1:12; 2:11; 4:21; Matthew 18:6; 27:42; Mark 1:15; 9:24, 42; Luke 22:67; 24:25 to name but a few.

As you may be aware, the Catholic position on *pistis* was that of the Latin *fides* – an assent that certain things were true: for example the church's teaching on salvation, coupled by striving to live a life in conformity to that teaching, helped by the saints with Christ himself as the great example. The great discovery of the reformation on *pistis* was that its meaning more closely parallels that of *fiducia* – trust.[13] Faith is the 'response of trust', itself a gift from God, so that faith might not be seen as a work. When Paul for instance speaks of Abraham's faith in Romans 4:3, 5, 18 and 20, it is this trust in the promises of God that he categorises as faith (verses 13, 16). It is this same trust that he has in mind when he speaks of faith in Jesus (verses 22–25). The Gospels denote this faith in Jesus by the frequent examples of people who helplessly turn to him for assistance, trusting that Jesus can help – and so, in fact, he does as in John 9.

Implicit in this biblical understanding of the nature of faith is an intensely relational dimension. Faith brings you into relationship with the one who promises, so that the focus is not just on the promises themselves, but on the one who promises. Again Jesus' own words in John 5:39–40:

> 'You search the Scriptures because you think that in them you have eternal

---

12. Where *pistis* is found in the Gospels, it is variously linked with belief or trust in the Lord's help in times of distress, and therefore could still be rendered as faith in an active sense – 'believing'. So Matthew 8:10; 9:2, 22, 29; Mark 2:5; 4:40; 5:34; Luke 5:20; 7:9, 50; 8:25, 48; 17:19. See Arndt and Gingrich (eds) *A Greek-English Lexicon of the New Testament* (Chicago: Chicago Press, 1979), 662–663.
13. For a helpful analysis of this difference, see J. Kleinig, 'Faith and Reason', *Interchange* 26 (1980), 90–96.

life; and it is they that testify on my behalf. Yet you refuse to come to me to have life.'

The Reformed position on faith is the belief in the Scriptures' testimony concerning Jesus Christ, and the coming to him as a result. A writer who I think has captured and expressed this relational dimension to faith better than most is Bruce Larsen. Author of a number of books,[14] he is widely regarded as the father of relational theology in the United States. Perhaps his most penetrating analysis of faith from a relational perspective is found in an interview that he gave to explain the rationale for his ministry.[15]

The background to his understanding of faith is the superficiality of 'fellowship' encountered by most Christians when they attend church, evidenced in the shock he experienced when one of his parishioners felt unable to tell him about the real struggles going on in her life. As Larsen says:

> Suddenly it hit me. That's what is wrong with the church in our time. It's the place you go when you put on your best clothes; you sit in Sunday School, you worship, you have a meal together – but you don't bring your life!! You leave behind all your pain, your brokenness, your hopes, even your joys.[16]

This lead him to ask the question of what it really means to have faith in Jesus Christ and belong to his people. It is in answering this question that he explores the relational dimension to faith.

> You see Jesus asks us three questions when we come to him. They are not true or false questions, they are yes or no. Lots of people say 'true' to the atonement, the resurrection, the second coming, but that's like saying 'True, I believe in marriage. Not until you say 'yes' to a person are you actually married.[17]

Larsen develops the theme of faith as personal surrender.

> So Jesus' first question is not 'Do you believe in the concept of discipleship'. It is rather this 'Will you trust me with your life, yes or no?' That's what he said to the disciples 'Will you leave the familiar, quit your job, pack up your goods and come along? Will you trust me in this?'[18]

---

14. To my knowledge he is still pastor of the University Presbyterian Church in Seattle, Washington. A selection of his titles include *No Longer Strangers, The One and Only You* and *The Relational Revolution*.
15. B. Larsen, 'None of Us are Sinners Emeritus', *Leadership* Vol 5/4 (1984), 12–24.
16. Larsen, 14.
17. Larsen, 14.
18. Larsen, 14.

Faith may be about saying 'true' according to Larsen, but it is even more about saying yes to a person, Jesus.

> Next Jesus asks, 'Will you entrust yourself to a part of my family, yes or no? Will you as an act of faith in me, entrust yourself to my people?'

Though the people of God may be better or possibly worse than he is, the individual nevertheless entrusts himself to them as an outworking of entrusting himself to Christ.

> Finally Jesus says 'Will you get out and be involved in my world? Will you try to walk my Word, my love, my character to somebody? Will you lose your life for my sake? Yes or no?'[19]

For Larsen this is the relational expression of faith in life. He comments:

> Years ago Johannes C. Hoekendijk wrote much the same thing when he portrayed the kingdom of God with three New Testament words. *Kerygma*, the proclamation that Jesus is Lord, *koinonia*, the family fellowship and *diakonia*, our service to the world. When people say 'yes' to all three we have an alive church.[20]

For Larsen the key dimension to faith is 'saying yes' that is, **surrender**, to give up on the pretence that 'I can run my own life' or that 'I don't need others' or that 'We are sinners emeritus'. Yet it is also **commitment** not to a set of ideals or ethical principles or codified laws but to the **Person** who makes forgiveness and restoration possible, the one who calls us to himself and to his people and so to be his salt and light in the world.

It is entirely possible to be critical of Larsen at a number of points, perhaps more for what he does not say than what he does. I find it disturbing for instance, that he can discourse on faith without elaborating on the Cross. Nevertheless he has looked at faith from a relational perspective and I believe given us some genuine insights as a result. Again I hope it can be seen how this relational perspective on faith has great potential for directing and shaping youth ministry. If our theological framework for youth ministry has faith as a central tenet, then we could do a lot worse than talk about faith in relational categories. This may not say everything there is to say about faith, but

---

19. Larsen, 15.
20. Larsen, 15.

it will say a great deal. The relevance to youth should be obvious. It is not simply to reinforce what they understand about personal commitment, friendship and trust – issues that are very much to the forefront of adolescence. Rather its relevance is to radicalise their understanding of these things by questioning the foundations upon which people build their trust and commitments and in the process call them to a different way. It is to call them to a person in whom trust will never fail because of the foundation on which that trust is built. It is to call them to a people where pretence is not needed, for that is not the basis of acceptance. It is to call them to a life not validated by success or achievement or acquisition, but rather by the one to whom they belong. It is to acknowledge their concerns and offer radical solutions. These are real possibilities when considering a relational theology of faith as applied to youth ministry.

Mission (historical)

I want to turn briefly to the outworking of relational theology in its impact on emergent youth ministry.[21] Adolescence as a distinct social and physical movement owes its origins to the Industrial Revolution of the late eighteenth and early nineteenth centuries. This dramatic period of economic and social change began in England and the Continent well before the United States. Children were employed in factories and young people migrated to the cities to obtain jobs that were no longer available in the rural areas. Men like Robert Raikes were concerned about the social and spiritual welfare of this emergent group, and in Gloucester he popularised a ministry to children and youth that became known as Sunday School. This idea rapidly spread to the industrialised cities of Europe and North America. His mission to youth was primarily educational, to enable literacy, yet also moral, to raise up godly young people who would use the Bible as the basis of their life.

As the Industrial Revolution continued, concern was expressed by leading Christians and the churches for the young people who had left families and migrated to the cities in search of jobs. Housing was awful and sexual temptation everywhere, with crime and violence

---

21. Those wishing to read more in this area will find Professor Mark Senter's thesis published as *The Coming Revolution in Youth Ministry* (Wheaton: Victor Press, 1992) especially informative.

unavoidable. To evangelicals this emergent youth class needed redemption, a focus for their lives, and guidance at a social, physical and spiritual level.

George Williams was a prime mover in responding to that need. A dry goods merchant, he began a Bible study for apprentices, clerks and young male assistants in that industry. From this modest beginning in 1841 came the founding of the YMCA. Commencing in London in 1844, this ministry spread rapidly to the Continent and to North America. It is important to note that the original objectives of this movement were distinctly Christian. Bible studies, prayer meetings, training classes for youth leadership were its main objectives though not at the expense of social and physical needs. It aimed to produce healthy minds and bodies for Christian service.

With social and economic prosperity, the industrialised nations developed a middle class and an emergent youth culture. Just how instrumental Christian youth organisations were in the formation of youth culture is hard to say. They were, it seems, the first people to recognise youth as a distinct entity – long before the advertisers and music industry – and to respond to them at a spiritual and social level. For instance the Society for Christian Endeavour held a conference for Youth in 1895 in Boston, and attracted 56,425 delegates. The first book written on the young people's movement was published in 1917, and it was a book on youth ministry!!

Nevertheless it would be a mistake to think that youth ministry and indeed the youth movement were the orchestrations of organisations or committees. Rather they were the result of an apparent working of God in the lives of individuals scattered across the nations to give them a vision, a calling if you like, for young people. The vision was to see them come to Christ and in the process respond to their other needs. I haven't the time to consider the contributions of people like Howard Guinness, E.J. 'Bash' Nash, Billy Graham, Stacey Woods, Vincent Craven or our own Howard Mowll, Joan Ash and Neville Bathgate to the development of youth ministry at the time of emergent youth culture. We have been fortunate to learn from Archbishop Harry Goodhew something of Graham Delbridge's contribution to this ministry.[22] Because of their vision and passion for wayward and lost

---

22. Graham Delbridge Lecture, Sydney, 1996.

youth who were open to exploitation and abuse, and their desire to win them for Christ and set them in turn to the task of winning others, great ministries were set in motion, many still with us today. It was said of Howard Mowll that he was often found at the youth courts, and there prayed for delinquents that they might be redeemed.[23] *In other words it was their theology that drove them.* They understood Jesus to be passionately concerned with young people, and how life had dealt with them. Jesus said, lamenting the hardness of heart of his contemporaries:

> 'I thank you, Father, Lord of heaven and earth, because you have hidden these things from the wise and the intelligent and have revealed them to infants; yes, Father, for such was your gracious will.' (Luke 10:21)

These visionaries would not have translated 'infants' ('little children' NIV)[24] in a metaphorical sense, for they knew it was never the children and youth who rejected Jesus in the New Testament. While not arguing for a theological glorification of youth and childhood, they at least saw that youth and children bring a clear perspective to spiritual matters in a way that adults do not, their perception now 'clouded' by the distractions of career, mortgage, car, retirement, superannuation and so on. What mattered to these people was the young person's relationship to Christ, how the Cross had made that possible, how it gave them acceptance and assurance before God the Father. They were concerned with the consequent challenge for a young person to live the Christian life and witness to others. What drove them was not fear of social change or a desire to maintain churches, or even moral or educational concerns, though these all played a role. Primarily they wanted to win young people into relationships with Christ and see them dedicate their young lives to his service. Howard Guinness expresses this perspective more powerfully than most. I quote from a brief tract on the Christian life he wrote in 1936 while working for Inter Varsity Fellowship:

> Where are the young men (and women) of this generation who will hold their lives cheap and be faithful unto death. Where are those who will lose their lives for Christ's sake – flinging them away for the love of him. Where are those who will live dangerously, and be reckless in his service. Where are his *lovers* – those who love him and the souls of men more than their own reputations or comfort or very life?

---

23. This event was noted by his biographer M.L. Loane in *Archbishop Mowll* (London: Hodder and Stoughton, 1960), 216.
24. Greek *nepios*, literally child, immature, innocent.

> Where are the men who say 'no' to self, who take up the cross of Christ and bear it after Him; who are willing to be nailed to it in the college or office, home or mission field; who are willing if need be to suffer and bleed and to die on it?
>
> Where are the men of vision today? Where are the men of enduring vision? Where are the men who have seen the King in his beauty, by whom all else is counted but refuse that they may win Christ? Where are the adventurers, the explorers the buccaneers for God who count one human soul of greater value than the rise and fall of empires?
>
> Where are the men who glory in God-sent loneliness, difficulties, persecutions, misunderstandings, discipline, sacrifice and even death.
>
> Where are the men who are willing to pay the price of vision?
>
> Where are the men of prayer? Where are the men who, like the psalmist of old, count God's Word of more importance than their daily food. Where are the men who like Moses of old, commune with God face to face as a man speaks with his friend and unmistakably bear with them the fragrance of that meeting through the day?
>
> Where are God's men (and women) in this day of God's power!![25]

This is how youth ministry and indeed the youth movement has emerged in history. Evangelicals were the catalyst, their theology the driving force. A theology that is both personal and relational yet visionary – extending beyond the individual to the many.

The Cross

At the heart of any evangelical theology must be the Cross. It is not my place to elaborate the work of the Cross, but I am keen to share with you how the theology of the Cross can impact youth ministry. Indeed it already has, for the people mentioned above have pursued the Cross as the central focus for their proclamation and teaching. But how can the message of substitutionary atonement inform and direct youth ministry? My thesis is that it does, for the work of the Cross is relational at heart.

McGrath[26] among others sees the theology of the Cross as the crucible out of which reformation theology in its more popular tenants – grace alone, faith alone, Scripture alone, Christ alone – was born. Any

---

25. As quoted from *Sacrifice – A Challenge to Christian Youth* (London: IVP, 1950), 61ff.
26. A.E. McGrath, *Luther's Theology of the Cross* (Oxford: Basil Blackwell, 1985), 178–179.

theology of youth ministry must concur with this underscoring that only through the Cross can we come to a genuine and Christian understanding of God's dealings with humanity, including youth.

I believe a ministry centred on the Cross, with its emphasis on God's self revelation; Scripture; failure of self justification and human wisdom; faith; justification by grace and the nature of the Christian life will give youth ministry a life and direction under the Spirit that may indeed shake the world, for in the Cross alone God engages with us as persons to judge our sin and so transfer us from death to life.

John Calvin commenting on substitutionary atonement says:

> This is the wonderful exchange which out of his measureless kindness Jesus Christ has made with us. That becoming a son of man with us he has made us sons of God with him. By his descent to earth he has prepared an ascent to heaven for us, by taking on our mortality he has conferred his immortality upon us, by accepting our weakness he has strengthened us by his power, by receiving our poverty upon himself, he has transferred his wealth to us. By taking the weight of our iniquity upon himself (which oppresses us) he has clothed us with his righteousness.[27]

In short on that cross, the place he chose to go and die in our place, Jesus Christ takes away all the evil our consciences tell us that we have, and gives us every good thing our conscience tells us that we lack.

Any theology of youth ministry is valid only in as much as it focuses on and is directed by this great reconciling work whereby God has restored our broken relationship with himself and restored our humanity in the process. This is the only rationale for youth ministry that relational theology can give us. To wander from it is to abandon the priority of relationship, to hate people, to despise God himself who has given the Cross as the basis of our reconciliation and restoration as persons.[28]

Having said that it is also true that the achievements of the Cross of

---

27. John Calvin, *Institutes of the Christian Religion*, ed. J.T. McNeill; tr. F.L. Battles, LCC XX & XXI (Philadelphia: Fortress,1960), IV xvii.2; O.S. V 343.29–32, 344.1–6.
28. The consequences for our humanity of Christ's reconciling work are given helpful attention in an essay by Ray S. Anderson entitled 'Christopraxis: The Ministry and Humanity of Christ for the World' in *God In our Place: The Humanity of God in Christ for the Reconciliation of the World* eds Hart and Thimell (Exeter: Paternoster, 1989), 11–31.

Christ can speak to many of the concerns that modern youth may have – not simply by way of solution, but revolution!![29]

The answer to futility

Creation has been disturbed and thrown out of kilter with the coming of sin, and this therefore affects all of creation including our bodies and our work. We encounter not only physical decay and destruction, but the frustration commonly felt by the young who feel their elders have made a mess of society, often with good reason. But when it comes to their turn will they make a better go of it? Can they? Often youth subculture develops as a reaction against perceived failings and hypocrisy of the older generation, and they sense that the older generation, despite its technology and power and wealth, has failed to create a better world. In that sense they are in line with St Paul who sees a world shot through with futility (1 Corinthians 3:20). Yet the young are not free from that curse – the advertising industry, with its emphasis on glamour and beauty and sex in order to sell, panders to latent idolatry and narcissism in youth. The Bible writers pour scorn on idolatry as an exercise in futility (for example, Isaiah 44) in that idols not only give us nothing but take from us even what we have. Paul's summation of the world's futility is found in Ephesians 4:17-18, and his explanation for it is in Romans 1:21. A world where the knowledge of God has been rejected is a world where the meaning of life has been removed. In place of the knowledge of God, futility has taken over. Young people feel the latter without necessarily understanding the former.

There is redemption from futility (1 Peter 1:8). A price was paid for that, and coming to the Cross of Christ involves the abandonment of futility, taking in its place forgiveness, acceptance, access to the Father and purpose/direction. This is not so much the answer to futility as its removal.

The answer to ignorance

Many argue that education is the solution to humanity's woes, and indeed we all have benefited enormously from the advances that education brings. However we may be eyebrow high in degrees and

---

29. I am indebted at this point to the fine analysis undertaken by L. Morris in *The Cross of Jesus* (Grand Rapids: Eerdmans, 1988), 27ff. I have adapted and expanded it somewhat.

diplomas yet we are still knee-deep in blood. We have not created a better, more humane or just society simply because of educational and scientific advancement. All too often that knowledge has been turned to selfish or destructive ends. It does not necessarily benefit the young, the unemployed and those who may never enjoy an education or the rewards that education supposedly brings. We have this to say: in the final analysis it is not so much our knowledge, but God's knowledge of us, that is critical. 'For God is greater than our hearts, and he knows everything' (1 John 3:20). He calls us to saving knowledge of himself and indeed true knowledge concerning the things that matter. This knowledge gives life and produces love (1 John 4:7) and calls us out of ignorance into God's light (John 1). This saving knowledge is directly linked to the death and resurrection of Jesus Christ (Romans 6:9). Unlike worldly knowledge this knowledge is certain and sure – 'I know that my Redeemer lives!'(Job 19:25).

The answer to loneliness

In a somewhat paradoxical way, although human beings have never lived closer together (80% of the world's population is now urbanised), people have never been further apart. Some argue that loneliness is the biggest killer in western society, and as a medical practitioner I know that patients seeing me with a variety symptoms are in many cases suffering from the consequences of loneliness.

Loneliness and alienation are feelings young people readily identify with. Sadly for many they are worn down by these relentless feelings and end in despair. It might surprise you to know that Australia is one of the world's leading nations in youth suicide! At a time in history when youth, generally the most optimistic of our society, feel there is little hope and have a sense of abandonment or godforsakenness, then we need to bring them a sense of the presence of God. There is no other way to come at this than through the death of Jesus on the cross – in that moment of utter isolation and loneliness he cries out to the Father. Gethsemane tells us of the utter horror of this experience (Mark 14:33, Luke 22:44, Matthew 26:38), and the subsequent Scriptures tell us why it was necessary (Galatians 3:13). He experienced the full horror and naked terror of an atoning death, to spare us from utter forsakenness and loneliness such as our own experiences can only hint at. Through his blood our isolation and abandonment is ended (Ephesians 2:11–22).

The answer to sickness and death

In modern western society with drugs and HIV/AIDS taking their toll, few young people will have escaped the spectre of death. It would be unimaginable to believe it is not an issue for them. Matthew points out that the final answer to our problem with sickness and pain is to be found in the Cross (Matthew 8:16–17). There Jesus takes our pain and illness and deals with them, offering not a removal today, but a confident expectation that sickness and pain can never take away. In the same way, Good Friday is followed by Easter Sunday so that death is not the end. Rather it has been defeated and the life of the Christian is marked by dying and rising in sure and certain hope of what will be (1 Corinthians 15).

The answer to selfishness

Unfortunately it is selfishness that underlies much of the modern philosophy of relativism and indeed the New Age movement as a whole. They are thinly disguised ways of portraying the 'me first' philosophy of life. The way of the Cross stands in stark contrast, for it is the path of self denial, and with good reason. The Cross brings death to the old man and life to the new, because it involves dying and being buried with Christ (Romans 6) so that we might walk in newness of life (2 Corinthians 4:10). Set free from a life that is self-centred and whose end is death, young people are offered freedom, expressed not in license but in service – the badge of that freedom (Galatians 5:1).

The answer to guilt

Guilt features strongly in youth, sometimes for no good reason. It is often related to antisocial behaviour or rebellion within family relationships. Guilt over sexual matters may feature strongly. The issue may be not that young people's consciences are oversensitive in the area of guilt, rather that adults have so seared their consciences that they are no longer as sensitive to guilt as they should be! Guilt is a real and destructive force – the antidote is forgiveness and cleansing (Hebrews 10:19–23). The past is washed away, and we are purified. We are no longer bound by the past and a troubled conscience. His blood is more powerful than even a young person's memories.

Relational theology and the contemporary challenge

If you are ministering to young people it won't matter if their background is privileged or working class or even homeless. You are dealing with people whose lives are undergoing dramatic changes. Among the many who receive our message we will find the marginalised, the alienated, the lonely, the insecure and frightened. Those who for whatever reason labour under terrible guilt or wrestle with barely concealed anger or despair. Those who, like the prodigal son of Luke 15, feel there can be no place or future for the likes of them.

Not so. In the Cross of Christ we hear the voice of the Father overtaking them in the far country with the incredibly joyful message – all is forgiven, you can come home – come home!

Let what stands here at the heart of our theology direct the way we go about youth ministry. This much has been evidenced from Scripture and history. A commitment to the concept and outworking of relational theology in the areas of Faith, Mission and the Cross could provide the key to a creative and God-honouring ministry.

May any evaluation of our work with young people we undertake as a consequence help us develop a direction for youth ministry that goes beyond what is merely important, to what is life giving in the kingdom of God.

CHAPTER TWO

The Trinity, the historical Jesus and youth ministry

Angus McLeay

The historical Jesus and Trinitarian theology

He therefore that will be saved: must thus think of the Trinity. [1]

The Trinitarian faith is one of the most fundamental statements of Christian dogma found in the church creeds.[2] At the same time, of all the basic affirmations of the faith it seems especially enigmatic – or even distant from us – at a personal level. It is a metaphysical truth claim which appears particularly abstract, since it doesn't relate tangibly to our experience or practical observation.

As for young people, coming to grips with abstract metaphysical truth claims doesn't naturally flow on from six hours of Nintendo or Quake II, hanging out at a shopping centre, or even a trip to the movies. In contrast, it could be argued that among young people the person of Jesus, or at least what he may represent, resonates to a significant extent.[3] In a world where church matters less and less, Jesus still intrigues, particularly his place in history. Interest in the historical person of Jesus[4] has boomed in recent times – at both scholarly and popular levels. Countless books, magazine articles, TV programs and several major films have appeared in the last couple of decades focusing

---

1. Athanasian Creed, in *A Prayer Book for Australia*, (Alexandria: Broughton Books, 1995), 488.
2. The Apostle's and Nicene Creeds are set out in a Trinitarian formula; the Athanasian Creed deals at length with the Trinity; it is the first article in the Anglican church's Thirty-Nine Articles of Religion.
3. Quote from *The Age*, 18 April 1998; compare J. Dickson, *A Hell of a Life*, (Kingsford: Matthias Press, 1996), 9–11.
4. The term 'historical Jesus', as used in this essay, is intended in the broader, popular sense of the 'historical figure'; rather than in any technical sense. It means to take full account of Jesus' historical, cultural particularity without creating a false dichotomy between a 'scientifically proven Jesus' and a 'Christ of faith'.

on Jesus of Nazareth – the first century Jewish prophet/peasant/revolutionary/Son of God/Marxist/poet/charismatic preacher/holy man/magician/Messiah – take your pick. It seems that Jesus is popular by reason of being anchored in history, rather than floating in metaphysics.

How then, at the close of the second millennium, does an apparently abstract and heavily metaphysical belief such as the Trinity become meaningful for the lives of young people?[5] This paper will explore the possibility of its retrieval through its connection to the historical Jesus. Further, what implications are there for the church as it seeks to make the Athanasian Creed – 'He therefore that will be saved must thus think of the Trinity' – meaningful to young people once again?

The doctrine of the Trinity

The doctrine of the Trinity is a statement about the nature of God. Though some theology has sought to derive the Trinity from the concept of one God, the effect of this is to make the Trinity an appendix to the core doctrine of God. In other words, the most basic Christian doctrine of God becomes unitarian rather than Trinitarian. Against this, theologians have recently argued that the Trinity must be seen as a fundamental statement about who God is. Karl Barth, in particular, reasserted the pre-eminence of the Trinity for Christian theology. This was an outcome of Barth's theological method – taking revelation as a source for our knowledge of God, based on two premises: God is self-revealing and God is revealed in essence through his economic (revealed) relations.

The Trinity is a statement about the relations that form the essence of God's being, which are revealed to us (by God) through the activity of Father, Son and Holy Spirit. Those relationships aren't derived by metaphysical proofs but seen in the way God has related himself to us.[6] The Cappadocian Fathers' Trinitarian thinking also places the spotlight on God's revealed relations. The Cappadocian Fathers made the concept of persons the primary starting point for reflection on the

---

5. Colin Gunton argues for Trinitarian theology to become a focal point for Christianity's appeal to the unbeliever: *The Promise of Trinitarian Theology*, (Edinburgh: T&T Clark, 1991), 7.
6. However, Barth's approach to revelation didn't appear to resolve the connection between metaphysical truth (big 'T' truth) and history, one example being his refusal to accept historical evidence to verify the resurrection.

Trinity.[7] According to their approach, personal particularity, relations and distinctions are essential for any description of God. So recent discussion has made the revealed relationships of Father, Son and Holy Spirit essential to reflection on the Trinity.

It is not difficult, then, to regard the Gospels as primary sources for Trinitarian thinking. Where else are the relationships between Father, Son and Holy Spirit so explicitly and thoroughly revealed? As the Gospel of John declares, 'no one has ever seen God', but God's Son 'has made him known' (John 1:18; also see 1:14–17). The Synoptic Gospels (Matthew, Mark, Luke) have been the particular focus for studying the historical Jesus and they provide ample opportunities for looking at the interaction between Father, Son and Spirit. For the sake of space and in order to pay special attention to the historical Jesus, this essay will confine itself to the relations between Father and Son in the Synoptics, highlighting just one aspect of those relations.

One theme of the Gospels which appears to be central to the life and mission of the historical Jesus is that of 'rule'. It is expressed or involved in the titles associated with Jesus, in his acts of power, and in the crucifixion, resurrection and exaltation. The notion of rule is inescapable in the Jesus of the Gospels and the early church's understanding of him. It will therefore provide a good starting point for exploring the Trinity through the historical Jesus and his relationship with God the Father.

Rule, kingdom and the historical Jesus

Bi-polar rule

The notion of rule is developed in several ways in the Gospels, whether through Christological titles, demonstrations of power, acted-out prophecy, eschatological sayings, and so on. Of particular interest is the way in which Jesus' words and actions establish his own rule, and how that relates to God's kingship. Yahweh is the sovereign ruler of creation. None compares with him and certainly no one or thing is to be worshipped before him. Yet when Jesus teaches, such as about the Kingdom of God, this is both affirmed and modified. There appears to be two 'poles' of statements about the Kingdom of God, one ascribes it to God, the other to Jesus. In this way, the one notion of rule seems 'bi-

---

7. See Zizioulas, *Being as Communion*, (Edinburgh: T&T Clark, 1991), 131.

polar'. That is, it exists at two separate poles at the same time. Examining a few areas of the Gospels will demonstrate the situation.

Kingdom of God

The Kingdom of God is a central element of the Synoptic Gospels, and it is generally seen to be central to Jesus' mission, as Luke 4:43 records:

> 'I must proclaim the good news of the kingdom of God to the other cities also; for I was sent for this purpose.'

The Kingdom of God refers to God's effective rule. However Jesus is more than simply an ambassador or representative of the Father, with no inherent authority in himself. The Kingdom of God is described not only as belonging to God, but as having been assigned to Jesus:

> [Jesus speaking to the disciples] 'I confer on you, just as my Father has conferred on me, a kingdom, so that you may eat and drink at my table in my kingdom' (Luke 22:29–30).

Jesus has authority to give the keys of the kingdom to his disciples (Matthew 16:19); to announce God's intentions with the kingdom (Matthew 21:43); to allow people to enter or shut people out (Matthew 7:21–27); and the kingdom is said to *belong* to him:

> 'Jesus, remember me when you come into your kingdom' (Luke 23:42; compare Luke 22:30; John 18:36).

It is possible to read in this verse that Jesus is only a representative – for example, 'remember me when you come into the kingdom you are part of' – however the nature and extent of Jesus' authority in the kingdom makes this interpretation difficult. In this situation Jesus can authoritatively declare that the dying criminal will enter God's kingdom. It is an affirmation of Jesus' kingly status in the midst of his humiliation (compare the sign over the cross, Luke 23:38).

The Gospel writers find no tension between setting two 'kings' alongside one another. It could suggest that there are either two kingdoms or two sovereign rulers of the same kingdom. Yet there is one rule, and two poles represented and existing in Father and Son.

Allegiance

In his mission preaching, Jesus calls people to put God's kingdom first, for instance:

'But strive first for the kingdom of God and his righteousness, and all these things will be given to you as well' (Matthew 6:33).

At the same time Jesus demands radical, personal allegiance to himself:[8]

> Another of his disciples said to him, 'Lord, first let me go and bury my father.' But Jesus said to him, 'Follow me, and let the dead bury their own dead' (Matthew 8:21–22).

Entering the kingdom requires not simply obedience to the Father's will but recognition of Jesus' lordship:

> 'Not every one who says to me, "Lord, Lord" shall enter the kingdom of heaven, but only the one who does the will of my Father in heaven' (Matthew 7:21).

In this passage, interestingly, recognition of Jesus' lordship is assumed to come before obedience to the Father. As Jesus proclaimed and enacted the kingdom of God in Israel, he called for allegiance to God *and* himself.

Father/Son

The Father/Son relationship is related to rule through the Old Testament notion of the king as a 'son of God'. The clearest example of this is Psalm 2:

> I will tell of the decree of Yahweh:
> He said to me, 'You are my Son;
> today I have begotten you.
> Ask of me,
> and I will make the nations your heritage,
> and the ends of the earth your possession.
> You shall break them with a rod of iron,
> and dash them in pieces like a potter's vessel.' (Psalm 2:7–9)

This psalm was significant for the early church's understanding of Jesus (compare Acts 4:25-26; 13:33; Hebrews 1:5; 5:5; Matthew 1:1; Luke 3:22). To what extent Jesus understood his identity within this framework is a debated point among scholars. It is generally agreed that Jesus' understanding of himself as Son of God focused on personal relationship and conscious activities fulfilling his Sonship (for example

---

8. While many explain away the harshness of Jesus' demand, see M. Hengel for a defence of this as a call to personal allegiance of the highest order. *The Charismatic Leader and His Followers*. Trans. J. Greig, (Edinburgh: T&T Clark, 1981).

baptism, Matthew 3:13-17; transfiguration, Mark 9:2-12; clearing the temple, Luke 19:45-46).[9] He regarded himself as uniquely related to God in a way his disciples were not.[10] This relationship was intimate and personal (for example, Matthew 11:25-27). It was also marked by active obedience and submission.[11] This combination of highly unusual characteristics and activities should not be read in isolation from Jesus' broader mission and self-understanding. His identity as the Son of God was central to his self-awareness (as the Gospel writers emphasise) and it is most plausible to see a link of the kind made in Psalm 2 as expressive of Jesus' own understanding (even though he did not make this particular link[12]).

With this in view, Jesus' Sonship is critical to his destiny, saving significance and kingly rule. The temptation in the wilderness is not only Israel recapitulated, but 'something greater' than Israel proving obedience in the wilderness, that is, Jesus doesn't simply 'represent', he also is someone of unique status. With Jesus as Son of God, his death on the cross takes on a greater dimension as an act of God 'for the forgiveness of sins' (Matthew 26:28). Acceptance or rejection of him is primary to coming under the rule of God. The confession of the Roman centurion, 'Truly this man was God's Son!' (Mark 15:39) is the acknowledgment the entire Gospel of Mark calls for.[13] Following Jesus is obedience to the Son of God and thereby entrance into the kingdom of God (compare Mark 10:21-25; Luke 18:22-25).[14] As Psalm 2 demands, appropriate response to the Son assures his rule will not bring blessing instead of judgment (Psalm 2:10-12).

The Father/Son relationship and rule are interwoven. Jesus'

---

9. Also J.D.G. Dunn's assessment in 'Christology', *Anchor Bible Dictionary*, (New York: Doubleday, 1992), 1.981.
10. For instance he distinguished between the disciples and himself in reference to the Father, see D.R. Bauer, 'Son of God', *Dictionary of Jesus and the Gospels*, (Illinois: IVP, 1992), 772.
11. For an overview of this see R.N. Longenecker, 'The Foundational Conviction of New Testament Christology,' in *Jesus of Nazareth Lord and Christ*, Eds J.B. Green and M. Turner (Grand Rapids: Eerdmans, 1994), 473-488.
12. Jesus is recorded as having used Psalm 110, which is closely related to Psalm 2, in Mark 12:35-37; Matthew 22:41-45; Luke 20:41-44.
13. How the centurion understood *huios tou theou* (son of god) is secondary to this point; what matters is how Mark is using the confession, and it is clearly connected to the introductory verse, 1:1.
14. In Matthew Jesus is worshipped by the disciples as the 'Son of God', Matthew 14:22-33. This is often regarded as Matthean redaction, compare W.D. Davies and D.C. Allison, *Matthew*, (Edinburgh: T&T Clark, 1993), 2.496-497.

relationship with his Father is generally expressed in functional and personal terms in the Gospels. That is, he is close to his father (personal, unique) and an obedient son (functional). This relationship cannot, however, be isolated from his right to rule, the Father's kingdom and the co-regency of Father and Son.

Crucifixion

It is at the Cross that the notion of rule is most drastically put to question. Much conservative theology emphasises substitutionary atonement in its analysis of the Cross. A related but too often overlooked theme is the reign of God and Jesus.

The supernatural signs which surround Jesus' death point to his vindication by God (especially for example the tearing of the temple curtain, Mark 15:38; Matthew 27:51; Luke 23:45; also Matthew 27:51–54 [apocalyptic events]; Luke 23:44–45 [darkness]). The vindication of Jesus' identity and mission by God is only one side of the 'equation'[15] of God's kingdom. Since the nature of God's rule is seen in openness, suffering, vulnerability and loving sacrifice, Jesus' death on the cross is necessary for its inauguration.[16] Luke uses the term *dei* to express the necessity of Jesus' suffering according to God's salvific plan (for example Luke 24:25-27). The resurrection of Jesus into glory (his exaltation to universal rule) is basic to Luke's understanding of salvation.[17] As Mark shows, the kingdom of God dawns in the person and work of Christ (Mark 1:14–15). Jesus explains the nature of the kingdom as one of service, of which he is an example:

> 'For the Son of Man came not to be served but to serve, and to give his life a ransom for many' (Mark 10:45).

It is central to this saying that Jesus' death is part of the nature of the Kingdom (the statement is part of a discussion on rule in the kingdom of God, compare Mark 10:35–45). The suffering of Jesus is part of the

---

15. Equation is in inverted commas because unfortunately the death of Christ is so often reduced (by modern evangelism) to solving an equation based on the 'problem' of sin, with the Cross being the 'solution'.
16. Of course this does not exclude his life or resurrection, in which the rule of God dawns.
17. That is, if God 'balanced the books' of justice with Jesus' death, then why the importance of the resurrection, in particular the exaltation of Jesus? As Green notes, the exaltation is the explicit means of salvation according to Luke-Acts (eg Acts 2.33; 5.30–31; 10.43). See J.B. Green, 'The Death of Jesus' in *Dictionary of Jesus and the Gospels* (Illinois: IVP, 1992), 160–161.

fabric of God's rule and in this way God's own kingdom depended upon Jesus' passion.

Resurrection

The resurrection is the keystone of Jesus' authority and rule. As Paul declares in a summary of his gospel:

> [Jesus] who was declared to be Son of God with power according to the spirit of holiness by resurrection from the dead, Jesus Christ our Lord (Romans 1:4).

The claim that Jesus had risen from the dead is undeniably early in the Christian church. The oldest reference to resurrection is probably from 1 Corinthians 15:3–7. The formula used by Paul in verses 3–5 suggests a well known set of statements among early Christians. It is understood by Paul that Christ's resurrection means Christ has been given all power, authority and rule.[18]

> Then comes the end, when [Jesus] hands over the kingdom to God the Father, after he has destroyed every ruler and every authority and power (1 Corinthians 15:24).

Following his resurrection, Christ has received all authority and must bring all of creation fully into God's reign. Here we see that resurrection grants Jesus a particular reign. Yet Paul continues by expanding on Christ's resurrected rule:

> Then the Son himself will also be subjected to the one who put all things in subjection under him, so that God may be all in all (1 Corinthians 15:28).

Christ's reign operates in one form between his resurrection/exaltation and the consummation of creation in the new age. Once the new age is ushered in, Christ takes on a new form of rule in subjection to God. That is, Jesus' rule is not neutralised by subjecting himself to God. On the contrary, his reign is fulfilled by actively subjecting himself as the Son to the Father. God's kingdom is established through the reign of the Son, leading to the establishment of the Father's rule, that he may be 'all in all'. In resurrection and exaltation the rule of God is seen as a mutually beneficial, serving dynamic.

Results

What kind of distinction does it mean where Jesus as vice-regent with

---

18. This is also the meaning of Matthew 28:16–20; Acts 2:32–36; 5:31; Philippians 2:9–11).

God, is also God's Son? At the very least, obedience is implied. This means Jesus distinguished himself and therefore his place in God's kingly rule by means of obedient Sonship.[19] There is no obvious sense of tension in the Gospels where Jesus appears to submit himself to God. For some this indicates the historical Jesus never considered himself on par with God.

Jesus willingly submitted himself as a person in dependence on God but it is not necessary to expect the Father to 'submit' in a reciprocal manner. Since Jesus and the Father are distinct persons, the Father responds by entrusting his care and love to the Son. The mission and submissive obedience of Jesus hold the key to the Father's own purpose and rule (compare 1 Corinthians 15:24–28 above). Submission in this way doesn't necessitate a hierarchy of being. Rather it indicates their distinctive personhood – for the Son, submission; for the Father, entrusting his love, care and rule in the Son.

Jesus is raised to glory, to share the Father's glory. His resurrection and exaltation destine him to reign in glory with the Father. As Revelation describes, Jesus the slain and risen lamb of God is at the 'centre of the throne' of God (Revelation 7:17). Authority to rule is given to Jesus, and his rule is the reign of God. God the Father, Jesus the Son, and the Spirit rule mutually (although not interchangeably or symmetrically). As 1 Corinthians 15 explains, this is to bring to consummation the loving rule of God for the world. Once this rule is established over against every opposing authority, Jesus will actively submit himself under God's rule as the Son. The 'Kingdom of God', therefore, truly belongs to God – Father, Son and Spirit.

The Father and Son have distinction and are *other* than each other (though not *separated from* to suggest independence). However, there is also mutual and reciprocal dependence. The cry of abandonment by Jesus on the cross cuts both ways: it asks whether Jesus is really God's Son and whether the Son of God really has God as Father. The vindication of Jesus' life, message and death also vindicate God's plan (especially in Scripture) and therefore ultimately the nature of his rule.

---

19. Pannenberg, *Systematic Theology*, translated by G.W. Bromley, (Grand Rapids: Eerdmans), 1.310.

The Trinity and the rule of Jesus

The well-known Trinitarian theologian, T.F. Torrance, has made the comment:

> If the Father-Son relationship occupies a place of primacy and centrality in the Christian understanding of God and the world, and of the Gospel itself, everything depends on precisely how we understand the relation of Jesus Christ, the incarnate Son of God to the Father.[20]

The emphasis on Jesus as Messiah, his Sonship, his proclamation of the Kingdom of God, his awareness of his mission and particularly his death is fundamental to understanding his personhood and place in the Trinity. The rule of God in and through Jesus of Nazareth gives us insight into the nature of God's existence and relations (internal and external). Their rule is not simply coexistent, nor is it best explained as co-dependent. Jesus does not have merely a representative or caretaker role over the Kingdom. The rule of Jesus and God the Father is real, mutual and reciprocal, giving and receiving (not asymmetrically) in accordance with the particularities of their personhood: Father and Son. The best way to explain the rule of Jesus and the Father is in Trinitarian terms, what is known as perichoresis – their mutually indwelling existence.

Application to Youth Ministry

Communicating Trinitarian theology

The preceding section has been an apologetic for the Trinity by way of studying the historical Jesus. Apart from the basic content of the argument, it has also been an example of a theological method for unpacking the Trinity. As noted above, the person of Jesus seems more tangible and intriguing due in part to his place within history. This paper is seeking to 'retrieve' the Trinity by demonstrating its connection with the historical Jesus. What implications are there for communicating Trinitarian theology to youth? This section will begin by noting some problems with traditionally popular ways of communicating the doctrine, and then suggest some alternatives based on the above discussion.

---

20. T.F. Torrance, *The Trinitarian Faith* (Edinburgh: T&T Clark, 1993), 7.

Problems with traditional explanations of the Trinity

Trinitarian theology is often communicated in conceptual forms. It is often introduced as a difficult, mysterious, doctrine which we will never get our brains around, but we have to believe it because it is so foundational for the faith. This approach owes much to Augustinian theology, which, because of its ontology of persons (person is defined as a substance) sees the doctrine as a conceptual conundrum (that is, how can three substances also be one?).

Some of the popular analogies for the Trinity aimed at explaining the doctrine have reinforced the conceptual approach, which on its own tends to grow the gap between people and their belief. For instance, the Trinity is described in terms of water – liquid, solid or gas. Or in terms of light – heat, light, the sun. Someone has even proposed illustrating the Trinity as a cake – layers, slices, ingredients (the Father is the ingredients; the Son the layers [by which God comes down to us]; the Spirit the slices [by which he is passed around]).[21]

The problem with these analogies is not so much their adequacy as illustrations, but their effectiveness as vehicles for communicating the truth of the Trinity. They fail at two levels. First, they operate in a non-personal sphere. They express relationships, but not of a personal nature. This may lead to confusion or obscurity at a point where evangelicals at least have wanted to insist on something non-negotiable: God is a *personal* being. The fundamental doctrine of his being must also have a personal explanation. Secondly, they offer models which appear distant from the realities of personal relationships. Hence, there is a tendency to relegate the Trinity to a compartment of orthodox beliefs with little obvious practical application to life.

An analogy which overcomes the first hurdle, but perhaps not the second is to use love – lover, loved, love. This is a step in the right direction, since it operates in the sphere of relationships. However, on its own it is somewhat abstract, unless further explained and elaborated upon. One way of doing just that is outlined below.

---

21. See J.B. Boice, *The Sovereign God* (Downers Grove: IVP, 1978), 141, who does not recommend this as the best of illustrations.

An alternative way to communicate the Trinity

Alongside appropriate analogies and illustrations, the opportunity exists for making use of the Gospels to provide insights into the Trinity. The doctrine can be introduced in the process of unpacking the life of Jesus and how he related to Father and Spirit (and vice versa). This centres the doctrine in a more relational model. It also means discussing the doctrine as Scripture itself does, rather than 3rd–5th century church history debates. For example, what does the Gethsemane scene in Matthew's Gospel tell us about the Trinity (Matthew 26:36–46)?

Jesus specifically goes to the garden to pray to his Father, anticipating his imminent arrest and execution (Matthew 26:36; compare verse 38). For someone who expects to be crucified shortly it speaks powerfully about what is significant to him. In other words, at a moment of extreme stress, Jesus demonstrates the ultimate significance of his relationship with the Father.

It is an example Jesus urges his friends to follow (26:41). Note that Jesus urges them to pray to the Father for their own sakes rather than his. Jesus is able to focus on others in the midst of his own pressing need. This is the kind of outlook he maintains within the network of his intimate relationships with the Father and the Spirit. It looks outwards, rather than inwards; it expresses love to other people.

The scene does not, however, suggest Jesus going to pray means that he is resigned about his fate and saying his last words before being swept away in the course of inevitable events. Jesus is actively wrestling with the decision to choose God's will as against what he could desire for himself (such as escape, or another way to fulfil his mission, 26:39, 42). Jesus has his own will. He is dependent, but this does not detract from his personhood, identity or stature (he is not in a dysfunctional 'co-dependent' relationship).

Here Jesus' submission to God is active, empowering and freeing. The Son is not independent from the Father, but lives in dependence while still maintaining his own identity. Having submitted himself to God he is able to wake his disciples and boldly go to meet his betrayer and the climax of his suffering (26:45–46). The oneness of the three persons of the Trinity is expressed in their individuality as persons at the same time as affirming their inter-relatedness and interdependence.

The Gethsemane scene gives us insight into the character of Trinitarian relationships. It says that to be a person is to be in relationship with another person *in these kinds of ways*. As humans we can do this only in part and inadequately, perhaps the strongest expression being the marriage relationship where the **two** become **one** flesh (Genesis 2:24). However, in the being of God the reality to which we can only aspire is expressed in perfection and completion. In this sense our every relational act is tied into the nature of our being, as creatures of a Trinitarian God.

Insights for evangelism

Perhaps the lack of Trinitarian references in evangelism is related to a fear of 'confusing' people with a difficult, mysterious doctrine. However Trinitarian theology offers many powerful insights and possibilities for evangelism. For example, the Trinity provides a powerful analysis of the nature of sin. A Trinitarian faith claims not only that God is defined by his personal relationships, but that the creation is characterised by relationships which are intended to reflect God's own being.[22] Part of sin's effect is to subvert and dislocate those relationships.[23] As one evangelist defined sin, it is about 'busted relationships'.[24]

Trinitarian thinking takes us further, because not only does it see sin as subverting relationships, but suggests its outcome as 'dead' existence. Since relations *constitute being*, the nature of sin is understood as challenging our very existence. If we exist in and through our relationships with God, each other and creation, and those relations are distorted, fractured and alienated, our ultimate existence is challenged and questioned. To then speak of hell and judgment makes sense from this point, for it could be described as 'dead' existence.[25] It is not hard for many people to identify with feeling 'dead' in a relationship, or to be in dead relationships, or to be cut off and 'dead' to people with whom they desire relationship.

---

22. This point is often not made in popular evangelistic material. One possibility about why the relational nature of God is left out is that gospel presentations are much more focused on presenting a 'problem' (sin) which needs a 'solution' (Jesus' death) than on telling people who God is.
23. See Colin Gunton's *The Actuality of Atonement* for these thoughts. (Edinburgh: T&T Clark, 1988).
24. The Rev Drew Mellor in evangelistic address at St John's Anglican Church, Diamond Creek.
25. Typically hell is explained in strictly judicial terms, which, while not un-relational, does not emphasise the personal dimensions of judgment.

Practical Steps

- Begin a topic on the doctrine of the Trinity with a story/stories from the Gospels showing how the Father, Son and Holy Spirit relate in given situations.

- Build on this by continuing to refer to how Father, Son and Spirit relate as one being in the course of other Bible studies. Introduce Trinitarian thinking whenever looking at relations between the Father, Son and Spirit. What do they reveal about who God is?

- When speaking theologically about youth ministry (whether to leaders or kids) link relational concepts back to the examples of the divine relationships in the Gospels. For example, we believe we're all interdependent. There's no such thing as solo Christianity. Jesus never acted in isolation. He always relied on his Father and the Holy Spirit for every decision and action. If God's Son couldn't live without relationships, neither can we.

- The Trinity relates to a number of key areas of youth ministry, such as identity, authority, independence, individuality and outreach. How much better to be linking these issues back to the foundations of the faith. For example, developing concern for outreach is modelled in the community of the divine being. Although a perfect community, the Trinity reached out to include us in their communal life at unimaginable personal cost. The imperative for a youth group, far from being insular and self-content, is to reach out even at great personal cost.

- Evaluate youth ministry purpose/vision statements in light of the Trinity. How is the Trinitarian nature of God reflected in the youth ministry vision/purpose? Is there a link between this fundamental doctrine and what is being communicated as the core of the youth ministry? If there is no apparent link, or only a contrived link, what can be changed? Can leaders as well as committed young people see the connections between who God is as Trinity, who they are and what they're doing as a group of God's people?

- Do your evangelistic preaching, materials and ministry relate people to who God is, as well as what he has done? How is the Trinity reflected in explaining to people who God is, how the Holy Spirit can change lives and how he has been revealed in Christ?

Conclusion

This paper has only attempted to give a snippet of the possible implications the Trinity and the historical Jesus have for youth ministry. Hopefully better, more relational illustrations and analogies will become popular. Hopefully the Gospels will become a treasure trove for teaching the doctrine and it will not be put under Week 9; Sub-heading B; Point 2 – 'The Doctrine of the Trinity'. Instead the nature of who God is – Father, Son and Holy Spirit - will be unpacked and applied as young people make their way in a world of relationships and are drawn in to the life-giving embrace of the Trinitarian God.

Chapter Three

A theological model of youth ministry
Stephen Hale

Background

Anyone who attempts to lecture in the area of youth ministry, as I do, will be aware of the paucity of material in a published form. There are piles of 'how to' books floating around – 'Junior High Youth Ministry', 'Camping'. There are regular appearances of books of the 'Youth Today' variety. Each of these is worthy and serves a particular purpose. Most of these volumes are addressed to the broader youth leader market. When it comes to 'A Theology of Youth Ministry' there is very little that I am aware of to which I can refer my students.

We started teaching a Bachelors level course in youth ministry seven years ago. Our external accrediting Institution adapted a New Zealand syllabus which started with 'Youth today' and then moved to 'Youth in Society', before moving to look at particular areas of youth ministry. The course was overwhelmingly sociologically-based and was obviously a modification of a University Youth Worker course. We have subsequently revised the syllabi to address the need for a theological basis for youth ministry.

Within my own Anglican tradition, evangelicals have always been at the forefront of creative and dynamic work with young people. Yet, there is little written that provides a theological basis for what we are on about. I suspect this is largely because youth workers are great activists and because people don't stick at youth ministry long enough to reflect upon it.

Where to begin?

'Where to begin?' is an important issue for any academic study and is of critical importance for those of us who seek to train Christian youth ministers. What does the Bible say about young people? What does the Bible say about ministry with young people? Should we not be concerned to understand the mind and mood of young people today so we can best work out how to minister to them? If we decide that we want to start with developing a biblical framework for youth ministry, how do we develop that framework and what is its content? These are some of the questions that lie behind this paper.

The starting points commonly pursued seem to be as follows:

a. Developmental theories;

b. Sociology - youth in society;

c. Theological/biblical perspectives;

d. Practical youth ministry;

e. Christian education, and youth ministry as a subset of it.

As I have suggested, the material available in the area of theological/biblical perspectives seems to be either missing or pretty thin. My concern is to try to present a way forward for addressing this issue. We must aim at the integration of a biblical framework with a thorough understanding of the needs of young people today. However, if we don't develop an adequate biblical and theological framework, we will produce youth ministers who will be unclear as to what they are on about. They may be acutely aware of the social situation of the youth they work with, but not so clear as to what God would have them do about it. We need to take the Scriptures seriously as well as wrestling with our culture and how to respond to it. In many church contexts the latter is a lot less controversial than the former.

Youth ministry is not derivative, dependent on the primacy of non-theological disciplines. Neither is it synthetic, a conglomeration of those disciplines with a biblical gloss.[1] Youth ministry needs to take its rationale from the very nature of biblical theology, which is at heart relational.

The Bible and young people

One could argue that the Bible says very little about youth and youth ministry. The Bible doesn't contain any neat chapters which offer a direct systematic theology of youth ministry. There is barely a mention

---

1. T. Hunter, 'Taking the Bible Seriously' (Graham Delbridge Lecture), *Southern Cross Journal* Summer 1996–1997, 12.

of teenagers or youth workers. Adolescents weren't regarded as a significant group in the ancient world as they are today.[2] Yet the Bible is insistent that God is the God of the Child.[3]

Jesus was himself an adolescent and had to develop and grow into adulthood (Luke 2:52). Jesus encouraged the children to come him (Luke 18:15–17) and had to discourage the disciples from keeping them away from him. In the apostolic ministry in Acts, whole households were converted (Acts 16:30–34). Paul's letters were addressed to household churches that included children. It was assumed they were present for the reading of the Scriptures and Paul's letters, because he specifically addresses them in the household tables found in Ephesians and Colossians. Paul addresses younger leaders in his letters (1 Timothy 4:12–16) and young men and women as groups (Titus 2:4–8).

There is an indication in some of the passages that the period of youth was seen as a probationary or preparatory period. We identify youth as adolescence through to young adulthood. Paul was concerned about Timothy's youth as a leader, but he obviously wasn't a teenager. For the Romans, the period of adolescence began at seventeen and ended at twenty-eight. The period of youth was a time of space before accepting full adult responsibilities, to experiment and expand one's character and gifts.

It was also a time for achievement. The Bible records the successes of many young people – David, Samuel, Esther, Josiah and Daniel, to name but a few. The time of youth is one when great achievements and spiritual leadership are possible. God uses young people just as much as he does adults. We need to honour young people, nurture their faith, character and gifts and give them openings and opportunities.

The Bible isn't silent in talking about or identifying young people. We gain some valuable insights as a backdrop to developing a theology of youth ministry, but we need a wider view if we are to develop a more comprehensive theological model.

Biblical models

In seeking to develop a theology of youth ministry there are a range of

---

2. M. Ashton, *Christian Youth Work* (UK: Kingsway, 1995), 16.
3. Ashton, 19.

biblical models that one could start with. Some possibilities might be:
- The nature of humanity: What does it mean to be human?
- Jesus as our model: the Incarnation model
- Kingdom of God: the Transformation model
- Before and after: the Conversion/Discipleship model
- Apostolic ministry: the Teaching model
- The Relational model
- The Family Ministry model

Different groups are keen on different models. Many of the American para-church models which have been spread around the world are strong on the Conversion/Discipleship model. Navigators, for example, has a strong emphasis on discipleship. The Transformation model is strong in Christian Development work and has become the focus for various models of youth ministry. The Incarnation is a powerful motif for many. Stevens' book *Called to Care* uses the incarnation as the model for youth ministry and Jesus as the pre-eminent minister and model to be followed.[4] Pete Ward sees the incarnation as the motivating force behind the Oxford Youth Works program: 'The sense that there is a parallel between our activity as youth ministers and the life of Christ has been a constant source of inspiration for Oxford Youthworks.'[5]

I prefer to start with the nature of God's character as revealed, with particular focus on the Trinity as the theological basis for our involvement with young people. I want to propose, therefore, a Relational model because God is a God of relationship.

The character of God

Some of the key aspects of God's character that form a backdrop to our main focus can be briefly summarised in the following ways.

God is personal

God's self-revelation of himself in the Bible is as a personal being. God

---
4. D. Stevens, *Called to Care* (Grand Rapids: Youth Specialties, Zondervan, 1985).
5. P. Ward, *Relational Youth Work* (Oxford: Christian Relational Care, Lynx, 1995), 17.

is an 'I' not an 'it'. God doesn't have a body, but he has thought, self consciousness, exercises his will and expresses love.

The fact that God speaks and reveals himself indicates his personhood. The word of God is self-authenticating for it is a personal word addressed by God to an individual and therefore heard by that individual. God wants to communicate with us person to person. Only a personal God would be interested in revealing himself in order to enter into relationship. Our use of language to describe God himself is adequate because it is describing relationships which derive from the character of God revealed in the Trinity.

God is sovereign

God is independent and therefore not a dependent being, but is the ground of all being. He is immortal and has life in himself (1 Timothy 6:16; John 5:26). God is consistent within himself, yet immanent – omnipresent in his creation (Psalm 139:7–10). God is all-knowing and knows all things past, present and future (Isaiah 46:10). God is all-powerful – he can do all things and is the source of all power (Job 42:2; Jeremiah 32:17).

God is holy

God is distinct from every created thing, especially in that he is completely separate from sin and evil.

God is righteous

God is a just God and is bound to act justly (Genesis 18:25).

God is love

God is love (1 John 4:8). God takes the initiative to create a relationship of love with us (1 John 4:10). Agape is the self-giving love of God to those who don't merit this divine giving of himself (Romans 5:6–8).

God as Trinity

In the Scriptures, God is revealed as Father, Son and Holy Spirit. Each is God, but is a part of one God. They are three in one. The earthly disciples were strict monotheists (Deuteronomy 6:4, Mark 12:29). Yet they were forced to acknowledge Jesus as God (John 20:28). The early

Christians were compelled by their knowledge of him to recognise the Holy Spirit as God (Acts 5:3–4; Ephesians 4:30). The doctrine of the Trinity wasn't the result of speculative reasoning and philosophy. Their belief in the Trinity was the result of their experience of the Trinity.

No-one today recognises the Trinity by their own resources. It is a view of God that only becomes clear by reading the Scriptures and reflecting on how the Scriptures describe the workings of our relationship with God. While it may seem absurd to some or incomprehensible to others, it is the heart of the Christian faith. 'Through it we understand not only God's nature and his relationship to us, but our own nature and our relationships to one another.'[6]

Jesus was very clear in maintaining the Old Testament teaching that there is only one God (Mark 12:29). Yet God is revealed as the Father (John 6:27), the Son (John 1:1; 20:28) and the Holy Spirit (Acts 5:3–4). Each member of the Trinity is distinct, yet they are a tri-unity – they coinhere (John 1:18; 14:16). God the Father is personal (John 15:9), God the Son is personal (Mark 14:62) and God the Holy Spirit is personal (Romans 8:26).

The Trinity isn't some sort of conceptualisation or abstraction. It is drawn from the self-revelation of God in Scripture. We can learn a great deal from how the members of the Trinity describe their interrelationships with each other.

God is a God of relationship, because God within himself enjoys relationship. The Trinity tells us that ultimate reality is personal relationship. 'God is ultimate reality, and is the ground of all other reality, and yet God is not a single monad, or an impersonal absolute, but God is relationship.'[7] The characteristic of true relationship is other-person-centredness. God is good, God is personal, God enjoys, enters into, experiences relationship within himself. The relationships within the Godhead are characterised by other-person-centredness.

As we read John's Gospel in particular we get a remarkable insight into the inner workings of the relationship between Father, Son and Spirit. We read that the Father loves the Son and gives all things to him (John 3:35). The Father shows the Son all that he does (John 5:20). The Son always does what pleases the Father (John 8:29). The Son's obedience

---

6. D.B. Knox, *The Everlasting God* (Hertfordshire: Evangelical Press, 1982), 50.
7. Knox, 51.

springs from his love for his Father (John 14:31). The Son does nothing of himself, but as the Father has taught him (John 8:28). The Holy Spirit is self-effacing. He does not speak for himself, but as the Son has taught him. The Spirit glorifies Christ (John 16:13–14). The Father and the Son are united, One (John14:10). Jesus reveals the Father (John 14:7, 9, 10).

These references open up a unique insight into the inner workings of the Godhead. Jesus and his Father enjoy a relationship of love, unity, openness, trust and mutual respect. One puts the other before himself.

Similarly the Holy Spirit is self-effacing and seeks to put the spotlight onto the Son. The sort of qualities we desire in a relationship are evident in the Trinity – love, intimacy, disclosure, trust and putting the other before yourself.

It is in John 17 that Jesus gives us his fullest insight into his intimate relationship with his Father. Jesus gives to his disciples the words that his Father has given him. Jesus' followers were the ones that God gave him and Jesus had introduced them to his Father and his teaching. All that Jesus has was given by his Father, and all that his Father has belongs to Jesus. Jesus and his Father are 'one'. Jesus and the Father have a bond of unity which they share with each other and allow us to enter into. Jesus prays that they may be brought to complete unity to let the world know 'that you sent me and have loved them even as you have loved me' (John 17:23). The Holy Spirit is the means by which this unity is to be created and sustained. The Spirit's presence in a believer is the presence of Christ and the presence of his love.

Jesus clarifies the implications of the relational nature of the character of God in the final verse. 'I made your name known to them, and I will make it known, so that the love with which you have loved me may be in them, and I in them' (John 17:26). Jesus wants us and all other believers to experience and enter into the loving intimacy of the relationship within the Trinity. God loves the Son and they are one, and he wants us to know and experience the love of God in a relationship of unity. The relationship between us and God is made possible by God's self-disclosure of himself to his Son, who revealed himself to us through his word. As we hear that word today we are able to enter into relationship with the God who is relationship.

In various passages in the Epistles, the Apostolic writers are concerned to explain how the Trinity is at work in the outworking of our salvation. An example is Ephesians 1, where Paul teaches that God the Father initiated our salvation by choosing us and then by sending his Son. God, who loves his Son, brought about our forgiveness and redemption through the work of Christ on the cross. We believed when we responded to the word of truth, and were given the Holy Spirit to dwell in us as a sign of God's presence and the fulfilment of his promises both now and in eternity.

Humanity – made for relationship

Image bearers

Human beings were made to bear the image of God, in his likeness (Genesis 1:26). God has created us for relationship, because he is relational. Humans desire relationship because we were set up for relationships. Our desire for love, openness, communication, intimacy and unity all come from our being made in God's likeness. True relationship expresses itself in other-person-centredness, self-giving. Humanity was made for relationship with each other and with God.

Purposive

Women and men were made to be God's agents in tending for and caring for God's world. We were made to be purposive and to use the resources of the earth for the creation of community, for the sake of others.

Fallen

The fall is the expression of the rebellion of humankind against God and it represents the breaking of the true image of God in humanity. We are still image bearers. Sin has made relationships self-serving, lacking the love , kindness, faithfulness and purity that mark divine relationship. 'When we are deprived of relationship we experience loneliness – a terrible ache that reminds us we were never created to be alone.'[8]

Jesus shared our humanity

Jesus entered our world and shared our humanity. Jesus was the true image of God and lived life as a human being as we were intended to

---

8. Hunter, 13.

live (Hebrews 2:5–18). Jesus came as God's true and living word to enable relationship with God to be established. Jesus came to restore our relationship with God and to restore our true humanity (Colossians 3:1–11). Jesus also came to create God's new society, a people in true relationship with God and each other.

God made us for relationship with himself and each other, and has done all that is needed to make it possible for those relationships to be restored and re-established.

Towards a theology of youth ministry

Having explored the character of God as a relational being who made humankind to enjoy and enter into relationship, we are now in a position to propose a theological model of youth ministry.

Relationship is the key

Young people are made for relationship, because God set them up that way. Most young people are preoccupied with friendship and relationship. Young people have more time available for relationships and have a wider circle of relationships than at any other point in their lives.

Young people are in transition relationally – from dependence to independence and from seeing self in family to seeing self individually and in the context of their peer group.

Youth ministry must be relationally oriented

As God has reached out to establish relationship so should we. As God revealed himself and was open in relationship, so we need to seek to be open and real with young people. As God exhibits true love so we must seek to exhibit and foster true love – other-person-centredness.

Youth ministry involves entering the worlds of young people

As Jesus entered our world, youth ministry involves entering the world of young people, being where they are, meeting them on their turf, entering into their personal and emotional world. Youth ministry will not happen just at the church, but in the world of young people. As Jesus suffered and died for us, youth ministry will involve suffering, struggle and self-sacrifice.

Youth ministry involves communicating the gospel verbally

As God communicates in words in order to make himself known, so we must reveal him to young people through speaking his words. God desires person-to-person relationship, and this is established and maintained through his words to us. You can't have a relationship with God other than through his word. As God sent Jesus to restore relationship we must present Jesus the person, Jesus the Saviour and Jesus the model of what it is like to be human – a model of true humanity and other-person-centredness.

As God desires relationship with young people, our primary role is to enable young people to know God and to be able to relate to him as God.

Youth ministry – restoring the image of God

The issue of identity is significant for young people. Youth ministry involves helping young people to discover who they are and what God intended in the first place. In Christ young people can discover who they are in a non-self-centred way. Growth in maturity involves growth in Christlikeness. Even young people who do not embrace Christ in their lives will be enriched by being a part of and near to God and his people.

Youth ministry – creating community

Relationship is meant to be experienced in community. As God is community within himself, God made us to enter into and enjoy community with him and with each other. Community-building needs to be intentional in a fallen world. Community-building will be expressed in a range of ways and contexts. As young people enter into community, it is a powerful context for discovering who they are and their unique giftedness.

Community with young people starts with youth and extends to adults. The church is God's new humanity/community – it is multi-racial, gender inclusive, its goal will be to be intergenerational but it may not start that way. It is the context for worshipping God (vertical) and relating to each other (horizontal).

Community needs to be re-expressed and restructured as a youth ministry grows and develops.

God's community is eschatological – a new community is being formed now, which is a foretaste of that which is to come.

Youth ministry – leadership in community

Jesus built a team and released them to reach the world. The apostles worked in teams when they went on mission. Jesus' team was made up of a diverse mix of people. Jesus and his core team attracted a large team of associates (up to 70). The apostles planted churches and appointed local leadership to continue the ongoing ministry and outreach.

Youth ministry must be done by a team of leaders who have an intentional level of community between themselves. There is no place for the maverick solo leader who wants to focus the ministry on him/herself. This style of ministry doesn't model Christ or enable young people to move into God's new community. Youth leadership teams model community and enable growth into Christlikeness for the youth leaders. Youth ministry teams need to be diverse to be able to relate to and include a diverse range of young people.

Youth ministry teams enable youth ministry to grow and develop both numerically and in terms of the range and diversity of ministries offered.

Youth ministry – a critical community

The experience of young people of Christian community, at a critical point in their lives, will shape their ongoing walk with God and involvement with God's people. If we want to grow and transform the church, we need to make a priority of working with the group that is most available, most idealistic and most visionary. The potential both now and in the future is critical and exciting.

Youth ministry – an inclusive community

True community is not exclusive, but inclusive, open to outsiders, drawing them in, attracting and absorbing more within itself. True community will be open to and attractive to the lonely, lost and marginalised. True community will be a place of refuge and hope for the many young people who come from dysfunctional family backgrounds in our society.

Youth ministry – a transitional community

Youth is a transition on the way in life.

Youth ministry will seek to impact and transform young people into maturity in Christ and assist them into ongoing adult involvement with God's people. Youth ministry is necessarily a transitional community.

Conclusion

We need to seriously wrestle with God's revelation of himself to us if we are to more fully develop a theology of youth ministry that is honouring to God and that will best serve his church. A relational model of youth ministry arises out the very character and nature of God and us as his image bearers. It fits with the developmental issues and needs of young people. It is a model offering hope for youth living in today's fractured post-modern world. From my experience in various settings it is a powerful, exciting and eminently practical model and vision of youth ministry.

CHAPTER FOUR

Developing persons in the local church
Mark Leach

The aim of this paper is to illustrate how a Trinitarian personalism translates into practice in the formation of community in the youth and young adult ministry at St Hilary's Anglican Church, Kew, Victoria. I will proceed by outlining the biblical and philosophical framework behind our approach to ministry, and then sketch our strategies for accomplishing our goals.

A biblical theology of Trinitarian youth ministry

The mission statement of St Hilary's is 'To lead people to a mature relationship with Jesus'. What this means is that the goal of our ministry is not simply attendance by young people at programs (bums on seats), but to see people's lives transformed. Locating this mission statement in the context of a biblical theology, I see our mission as helping young people become truly human.

Humanity created

In Genesis 1 and 2 we see human beings created in the image of God. There are a variety of ways of understanding Genesis 1:26–28 and the exact nature of the *imago Dei* and I do not propose to argue for any one particular understanding.[1] What does emerge with great clarity from Genesis 1 is that relationships are at the heart of what it is to be human. God made humankind with the capacity to relate to himself, to other humans and to the creatures and creation. In Genesis 2, the account of the garden of Eden puts before us the picture of humans existing in a web of whole, perfect relationships. Out of their relationship of trust and obedient dependence upon their creator

---

1. For a stimulating overview and discussion of these see the article by K. Vanhoozer, 'Human Being: Individual and Social' in C.E. Gunton (Ed), *The Cambridge Companion to Christian Doctrine* (Cambridge: Cambridge University Press, 1997).

(2:15–17), everything else flows naturally, climaxing in the picture of total intimacy and community between the man and the woman (2:24–25).

Humanity distorted

Genesis 3 recounts the story of humanity's rebellion against its creator and the subsequent fracture of the relationships outlined in Genesis 2. As a result of this rebellion, humankind is now separated from its creator, from each other and from the goodness of creation. Relationships are no longer unambiguously good; all contain within them alienation, pain and frustration. Shame, self-centredness, separation and death now thwart God's intention for human community.

Humanity restored

The rest of the Bible is the story of how a faithful creator sets out to restore the relationship of love and obedience between himself and his creatures, and so to undo the effects of human sin and bring his blessing and order to the chaos of the world.[2] In the Old Testament this plan revolves around the creation of a people whom God will bless and through whom he will act to bring blessing to all nations of the world (Genesis 12:1–3). However, the nation Israel fails to be God's people. They continue the sin of Adam, and so God sends his own Son Jesus, to be the one true human person who will live, die and rise again to make possible the reconnection of humanity with its creator (Romans 5:12–21). There are now only two sorts of human beings: those who are in Adam and those who are in Christ. Those who are in Christ are those who by faith and through the Spirit have been joined with Christ. With Christ they now have before them the hope of a renewed reality where they will inherit the glorious freedom for which humans were originally created (Romans 8). From this position, we can add to our discussion of what it is to be made in the image of God and say that

> to be in the image of God is to be created through the Son, who is the archetypal bearer of the image. To be in the image of God therefore means to be conformed to the person of Christ. The agent of this conformity is God the

---

2. W.J. Dumbrell, *The Search for Order: Biblical Eschatology in Focus* (Grand Rapids, Michigan: Baker Books, 1994), 15–35.

Holy Spirit, the creator of community. The image of God is then that being human which takes shape by virtue of the creating and redeeming agency of the triune God.[3]

The purpose of our ministry is firstly to give as many young people as possible the opportunity to come to Christ through the proclamation of the gospel and so move from death to life. Secondly our purpose is to disciple and teach those who are in Christ so that more and more their true humanity can be expressed and shaped, for the glory of God and the blessing of others.

Humanity expressed

The life to which we are inviting young people is not a life lived in isolation. There is no such thing as a solitary Christian. In Christ we are those who are in the community of God's people. This community is to be in this world an echo of the divine community of the triune God. The path of discipleship is the journey to becoming the sort of person who has the character to express in relationship with others the same other-person-centredness that God displays towards us.

How does this happen? Paradoxically, the ability to create community happens in and through community. There is a Xhosa saying that captures the essence of a biblical anthropology, *umuntu ngmuntu ngabantu*, which translates as something like, 'persons are persons through other persons'.[4] Ultimately it is from the person of our Creator that we owe our existence as persons. Our personhood is made to be related to our creator. This is the telic end for which we are made.[5] Our personhood also depends on human, embodied persons. Without the persons of our parents we would not physically exist, and without the love and grace of the church community we would not exist as spiritual persons. Without being loved, we cannot love. Without receiving grace, we cannot be people who extend grace.

Some theological assumptions

The question to be addressed is: how do we set up a ministry that is most effective in helping young people live out their identity and

---

3. C. Gunton, *The Promise of Trinitarian Theology* (Edinburgh: T&T Clark, 1991), 117.
4. A. Shutte, *Philosophy for Africa*, (Milwaukee, WI: Marquette University Press, Reprint Edition October 1996).
5. O. O'Donovan, *Resurrection and Moral Order: An Outline for Evangelical Ethics* (Grand Rapids: Eerdmans, 1994).

humanity in Christ? Before we discuss some of the practical strategies we use to achieve this goal of transformation, I will make explicit a couple of key theological assumptions that flow from our biblical theology and that will underpin our strategies.

The priority of the Word

Proclamation and teaching of the Bible will be both formally and materially fundamental to Trinitarian youth ministry. At the heart of what it is to be in relationship – in community – is communication. To paraphrase Barth: God's being is being-in-communicative-act.[6] It is through his Word, incarnate and written, that God reveals himself to us and acts to draw us into relationship with himself. Without this ministry of the Word it is impossible to create a community that expresses true humanity. The human creature does not live by human community alone but by 'every word that comes from the mouth of God' (Matthew 4:4). It is the Word of God which is powerful to transform, recreate, shape and mould our young people (2 Timothy 3:16–17). A concern for community and Bible teaching are in no way mutually exclusive. In fact, the best teaching of the Bible happens in community at the same time that it creates community.

It is from the Bible that we get a vision of what it means to be truly human. This is the vision of true humanity that we must cast before our young people with the challenge to become people who are radical lovers of God and of other people. The Bible paints very clearly the despair and futility of a life that is spiritually autistic, turned in on itself, seeking first and foremost life on its own terms.[7] While our culture exalts the stories of individuals meeting their own needs, the Bible wants our young people to have lives that tell a wholly different story – a story of self-sacrifice, self-giving and servanthood. It is the Bible alone that gives us the assurance that these are the only stories with the guarantee of a happy ending (Revelation 21–22). If the Bible is not taught to young people in a way that is relevant and engaging they cannot possibly have the vision, motivation and hope to become people who can give themselves in community in a way that will echo God's self-giving.

---

6. Vanhoozer, 178.
7. Vanhoozer, 177.

The role of the Spirit

The Spirit of God operates to give faith, to unite people to Christ through the proclamation of the Word, to draw people into the community of the Godhead. The Spirit also shapes the new order of existence in people. Through the Word of God and the people of God, the Spirit works to transform people, so that the community of the church becomes a taste of heaven for a watching world. As part of this role, the Spirit gifts the people of God with gifts to serve and bless others. Every person who is in Christ has the Spirit of Christ, and has gifts from the Spirit which must be identified and released into ministry to bless the community. Age is no barrier to the operation of the Spirit, and one of the keys to successful youth ministry is encouraging young people to discover and use their gifts to minister and serve each other. After all, the best person to evangelise a young person is another young person with the gift of evangelism.

A Strategy for Trinitarian Youth Ministry

The priority of leadership

A central implication of the kind of Trinitarian personalism we are developing is that leadership is absolutely critical. It is the quality of the leaders of any youth ministry that will determine the kind of young people who are produced by the ministry. Insights from family systems theory tell us what is intuitively obvious: the emotional, relational, spiritual and psychological health and wholeness of the leadership community will be lived out among the young people they are leading.[8]

One of the implications of the importance of leaders is that volunteer leaders must be seen as the most valuable resource the church has for fulfilling its calling to disciple young people. Time and effort and love and training must go into the lives of the leaders. In particular we must continually be encouraging our leaders to attend to their own growth and development as whole persons; emotionally, spiritually, relationally,

---

8. Two very helpful books on this issue are, W.R. Richardson, *Creating a Healthier Church: Family Systems Theory, Leadership, and Congregational Life* (Minneapolis: Fortress Press, 1996) and E.H. Friedman, *Generation to generation: Family Process in Church and Synagogue* (New York: The Guildford Press, 1985).

sexually.⁹ For this to happen the team leader must work hard to develop a culture of trust and care within the leadership team. The priority on relationships must be reflected in the team leader's allocation of time and emotional and physical resources.

There is one crucial area of training and education which in my experience is often neglected in youth ministry, and that is helping the leaders understand the nature of their own ego boundaries, and how to maintain healthy and appropriate boundaries with the young people they are discipling. In practical terms this means things like helping a moderately needy and dysfunctional twenty-something deal with being the object of a young, vulnerable, needy person's infatuation. Part of this training needs to include helping leaders understand the processes of transference and counter-transference.[10]

Many problems and much damage to young people can be avoided with a rigorous screening process for leaders. Many people are attracted to youth ministry by their own emotional neediness. While there certainly is a place for such people, it is definitely not where they can shape and influence the personhood and character formation of young people. At the very least every leader should have a rigorous interview before taking up leadership. References should be provided, and, where possible, a police check conducted. Having been through this process, each leader must consent to a code of conduct, where relational and sexual boundaries are set, and must then be held accountable to that code of conduct.

> **St Hilary's Anglican Church Volunteer Leaders code of conduct**
> I will endeavour at all times to conduct myself in a manner that honours God and His Church. In all financial matters I will act with scrupulous honesty and publicly account for all monies handled by me on behalf of others. I will endeavour to conduct all my personal relations in a godly manner, acting with respect, love, integrity and truthfulness toward all those with whom I associate, irrespective of position, race, gender or religious opinion. I will seek to pursue reconciliation when conflict or division occurs. I will seek to be truthful, actively avoiding exaggeration, misrepresentation or gossip. I will practise Christian standards of sexual morality in all my personal relations and

---

9. These two paragraphs appear in similar form in my recent lecture *Sex, Lies and the Church: Developing Sexual Character in Young People,* Ridley College, Peter Corney Lecture in Youth Ministry, 1998.
10. One of the most helpful resources I have come across for dealing with this matter are the lectures that Arch Hart has given at Ridley College on a couple of occasions.

agree to uphold those standards in my teaching and discussions with young people at St Hilary's; particularly as expressed in the statement by the Melbourne Anglican Synod 1993, that 'This Synod: re-affirms the Christian standard of faithfulness within marriage and chastity outside marriage.'; and the statement on homosexuality approved by the vestry of St Hilary's Kew in 1993 (available through the church office). I will actively promote a safe environment where sexual harassment or abuse are neither tolerated nor able to take place undetected. I will not enter into any relationship, emotional or sexual, with any young person associated with St Hilary's, while I am in any position of leadership at St Hilary's, that is inappropriate or illegal in terms of age or power differences.

The importance of a system

Having established what it is we want our young people to become, and having recruited the right sort of volunteer youth leaders, we need to understand how it is that we will lead young people to the place of maturity in Christ. It is vital to have a system in place that makes clear in a series of logical steps what type of ministry needs to be directed to people to move them forward. The move from unchurched, self-centred neo-pagan, without God and without hope in the world, to young urban missionary whose life is totally oriented around serving God and serving other people (see Ephesians 2) does not generally happen in one step. In my experience, most youth ministries, and churches, have no clear idea about the path people need to be guided on in this journey. With some games, the odd camp, guitar music, a few Bible studies and a bit of luck they hope somehow God will do his thing and young people will stick with their decision to follow Christ and end up mature.

To understand the process we use at St Hilary's we must first outline how we segment our market. We see our youth ministry as being made up of five concentric circles:[11]

This model also helps us to see what ministries different people need. **Community** and **Contacts** need evangelism through relationships so that they can become committed to Christ and committed to membership of our **Congregation**. **Congregation** needs teaching and discipleship so that they will become people who are deeply committed

---

11. The following model and diagrams are adapted from R. Warren, *The Purpose Driven Church: Growth without Compromising Your Message and Mission* (Grand Rapids, Michigan: Zondervan, 1993).

Community = unchurched people within a 15 minute drive of St Hilary's.

Contacts = people with whom we have evangelistic contact through a relationship, an event, service.

Congregation = those who attend St Hilary's services regularly and who are committed to Jesus.

Committed = those who are committed to growing in spiritual maturity.

Core = those who are committed to the St Hilary's mission and vision, and living out the Great Commission and Great Commandment through the ministry of St Hilary's.

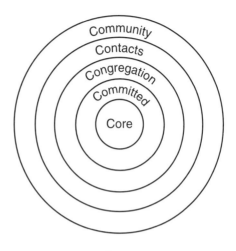

Figure 1

to Christian growth. The **Committed** need to be trained and equipped so that they can discover and use their gifts to live out the Great Commission and the Great Commandment in their lives, and so become part of our **Core**. People in the **Core** need to be supported, encouraged, loved and led as they go out into our **Community** to play their part in fulfilling the Great Commission through St Hilary's. This is shown in Figure 2.

This way of viewing our ministry means that we do not try to meet everyone's needs in every ministry. Rather we can clearly identify what each ministry is trying to do, and then ruthlessly evaluate whether or not that ministry is achieving its intended outcomes. For example, once a month our evening service is called Sunday Night Live. This is totally targeted at our Community and Contacts. It is effectively a multimedia evangelistic concert to which our Core members invite their unchurched friends. We do not expect people who attend to understand the finer points of Paul's argument to the Galatians, but we do expect that everyone who attends will understand what they must do to be saved.

The question may be asked of us, in what way is Sunday Night Live forming community? There is no intimate caring and sharing, no schmooze time, no emphasis on mutual encouragement. How then is it implications for every facet of Christianity and how we go about ministry into the next millennium.

Postmodernism has up to this point been viewed as what I will term a 'Spong' type problem. This problem derives its name from the Bishop of Newark, New Jersey, John Spong. Every couple of years Bishop Spong produces a new book that generates plenty of publicity in the secular press. The Christian community then becomes gripped by panic as it wonders how to deal with this new challenge to the faith. The walls of Fortress Christianity are challenged by an attack from 'out there somewhere' that threatens to breach them and demolish the faith. The normal pattern of events is for some Christian author to write a response which assures the reader that Spong is in fact wrong. The Spong type problem is dealt with by providing an intellectual rebuttal which shows that the walls are still very much intact and can more than adequately fend off the attack.

Postmodernism however is not a Spong type problem. It is not an issue that can be understood as a challenge to Christianity from 'out there somewhere'. A Spong type response may well be appropriate for some issues like New Age beliefs or a book on the Bible, but it is not an appropriate response to deal with the paradigm shift in worldview that is postmodernism. The postmodern shift profoundly affects every aspect of Christianity including worship, our attitude to the Bible, how we do theology and how we understand ourselves.

The focus of this paper is to highlight one example of the profundity of the postmodern shift by outlining the change from the modern to the postmodern concept of the self. I then want to consider the implications of this changed concept of the self for Christian ministry and for youth ministry in particular.

The modern conception of the self

To speak of the notion of 'the self' is to talk in a generalised manner about the characteristics of the self in an idealised form. The self can be defined as the essential characteristics of a person, his or her nature, way of thinking and outlook on the world. The concept of the self is very much a product of its age and arises out of the prevailing intellectual and cultural framework of the day. There is therefore a considerable difference between the notion of the self that arises out of

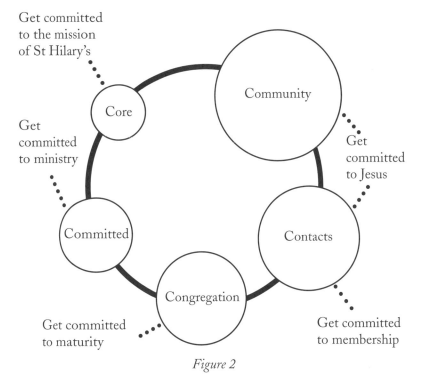

Figure 2

different to an ordinary concert? Profoundly so, I would reply. Sunday Night Live forms community by presenting the gospel to young people so that they can be drawn into Christ's community and start the process of incorporation and growth. It is the first step in the community formation process. Without it, you would have no disciples who could love each other!

The table on the following page illustrates how we target our ministries to meet the needs of people in each segment of our market.

Our vision at St Hilary's is to have a Core of 600 fully devoted followers of Jesus between the ages of 12 and 30 committed to fulfilling the Great Commission in their generation. To achieve this we have to make sure that we are effectively reaching enough people in each segment of our community and are moving them through the process. The model enables us to see where the bottlenecks are, and allocate resources to make sure that as many people as possible are moved into our Core. What we are trying to do is integrate a theologically driven

Community	Contacts	Congregation	Committed	Core
Christmas services	Earth Club (adventure camping)	Regular Sunday Services	Discipleship groups	Ministry Training Program[12]
School chapel	SNL	Camps	September Conference (6 day teaching conference)	Quarterly Leaders Meeting
	Outreach nights		Teaching Nights	
	Pub nights		Shape program[13]	
	Social nights			

vision of forming people in community with the most pragmatic and effective management system.

Conclusion

All young people are hungry for community and intimacy. Our goal for them is not **any** community, but rather a theologically defined community: those who are in Christ. At different stages of the process of maturity, this community will mean different things to them. At the start it is a community of people who welcome and accept them, and then through whom they hear the gospel. It then becomes a community which nurtures their faith and helps them become grounded in their relationship with their Creator. As this unfolds, the community becomes the context in which they are loved into greater interpersonal wholeness and begin to be people who recognise that they have gifts of the Spirit and a contribution to make to the good of the other. The community becomes the place where they learn to serve and to give, a place where a servant heart and character is formed. The goal is reached when young people have become community builders. Their lives have been so formed by the gospel that they are drawing others in, discipling others, and being part of giving a watching world a taste of the very love that characterises the love relationships of the triune God.

---

12. This is an intensive internship program which combines theological study, mentoring and leadership development in the context of various ministry experiences.
13. A gift identification program from Rick Warren.

CHAPTER FIVE

Youth ministry and the postmodern self

Andrew Stewart

Introduction: the shift to postmodernity

It will not come as any great revelation to you if I suggest that church is often slow to respond to change. Whatever the level at w change takes place, whether it be adapting to new social trends new music style, the church can rarely be said to be leading the This ongoing struggle to be relevant and cope with the rapid pa change is felt most acutely by those engaged in youth ministry. C is more often evident among the young, who tend to be quic respond to new ideas and trends than older people. Youth m must therefore be prepared to be at the forefront of facilitating within the church, in order to ensure that a generation of peop not feel that church has lost its relevance for them.

Sometimes the change is about seemingly trivial matters ensuring that one's illustrations for youth talks no longer Teenage Mutant Ninja Turtles. But in other instances the ch be of a far more profound nature. The paradigm shift in thin is required to embrace the postmodern worldview is one suc of profound change. While some Christian authors a advantage of the new buzz word by using postmodernism to latest book, it will be up to those of us who work among wrestle with this new challenge and to work out how it mission to young people.

This paper begins with a warning of sorts. The church is fai seriously the challenge offered by postmodernism. To ge reaction of the mainstream church, postmodernism is pe problem 'out there somewhere' that poses a challenge to minister to the group labelled Generation X. What they grasp is that the shift to a postmodern worldview ha the modern period, and the postmodern self that we are still struggling to come to grips with.

The modern self can be broadly defined by three general characteristics: being rational, autonomous and optimistic.

The modern self is a product of the Enlightenment where the key to humanity's progress was to be understood in the pursuit of rational scientific inquiry. Rigorous scientific methodology would eventually provide the answers to all our questions about ourselves and the world we live in, with most intellectual disciplines including theology embracing a framework based upon scientific principles. Scientific methodology was an important foundation for the modern self, as people believed that progress for an individual occurred when false notions and beliefs were discarded through a process of rational scrutiny of one's assumptions and worldview.

The second important characteristic of the modern self is individual autonomy. This is also a product of the Enlightenment, as the concept of the modern self began to emerge from the intellectual and social constraints of the Middle Ages. As educational opportunities improved, people no longer depended on imposed knowledge from external authorities, but could find out meaning, truth and value for themselves. They perceived that an important part of society's progress occurred when constraints to individual autonomy were eliminated. The modern self was characterised as a rational, autonomous, moral agent, capable of being in complete control of its own choices, values, and destiny.

The twin factors of rationality and autonomy combined to ensure that the overall flavour of the modern self was optimistic. Its faith rested on the assumption that life was an ongoing part of a continuing process of improvement and advancement, as we understood more about ourselves and the world in which we live. Once we understood, we could then begin to exercise control, using technology to overcome the obstacles to our progress. 'The modern self retained a basic optimism about the capacities of human reason, governmental or social strategies and scientific achievement, to shape the world for the general advancement of human society.'[1]

---

1. A. Thiselton, *Interpreting God and the Postmodern Self: On Meaning Manipulation and Promise* (Great Britain: T&T Clark, 1995), 12.

Richard Tarnas in his book *The Passion of the Western Mind* sums up the attitude and outlook of the modern self:

> And so between the fifteenth and seventeenth centuries, the West saw the emergence of a newly self-conscious and autonomous human being – curious about the world, confident in his own judgements, sceptical of orthodoxies, rebellious against authority, responsible for his own beliefs and actions, enamoured of the classical past but even more committed to a greater future, proud of his humanity, conscious of his distinctness from nature, aware of his artistic powers as individual creator, assured of his intellectual capacity to comprehend and control nature, and all together less dependent on an omnipotent God.[2]

The postmodern conception of the self

The shift to the postmodern worldview has seen the death of the modern concept of the self. The key defining notions of the modern self – rationality, autonomy, progress and optimism – have been replaced with cynicism, constraint, stagnation and despair. The postmodern self has lost faith in the modern idea that science is able to provide all the answers to life's problems and difficulties. It ridicules the optimistic notion of human progress, that a technological salvation from the human situation is possible. The idea of an autonomous humanity free of constraints is rejected as a naive and unobtainable ideal, as the reality for the postmodern self is being constrained by a whole host of competing forces and interests from which people can never hope to escape.

The postmodern self is very aware that people's lives are largely determined by forces totally beyond their control. While the modern self perceived itself as an active agent able to take control of its life, the postmodern self sees itself as constantly subject to the control and manipulation of others. 'Postmodernism implies a shattering of innocent confidence in the capacity of the self to control its own destiny.'[3]

The characteristics of the postmodern self include a loss of personal identity, and a profound loss of confidence in the self's ability to have any impact on the world. The postmodern self is fragmentary, uncertain, inconsistent and anxious. This profound insecurity and

---
2. R. Tarnas, *The Passion of the Western Mind* (Great Britain: Random House, 1991), 282.
3. Tarnas, 11.

cynicism manifests itself in an increasing preoccupation with defensiveness, self-protection and self-interest. The postmodern concept of the self provides a more honest assessment of a person's place and role in society than the modern self could. But this worldview is profoundly cynical, lacking in hope, and deeply suspicious of those who claim to monopolise the truth.

The postmodern self has become what is termed 'decentred'. There is no longer any core or centre to people to act as a foundation for their understanding of themselves and the world they live in. The result of this is that the postmodern self is adrift without a reference point or framework that can provide the anchor for its identity and belief structures.

One of the major contributing factors to the postmodern self's cynicism and distrust has been the collapse of the notion of truth. For the postmodern person, truth claims simply act as devices which attempt to legitimise claims of power.

> Postmodernists have given up on the 'game' of truth-seeking. They have recognised the not-too-subtle power dimensions involved in trying to define what is true. It is a smokescreen for deciding who's in and who's out, and who controls the game.[4]

Advertisements provide the perfect example of this, as everyone knows the claims they make are not claims based on truth, but are skillful attempts to manipulate the viewer to purchase the product. The use of force, manipulation and seduction has become more important in society than appeals to notions of truth. We see this trend with political disputes where the emphasis is not on setting up forums to encourage debate and discussion, but on setting up lobby groups to persuade and cajole.

The decline of the modern self has had a number of significant consequences, one of which has been the collapse of traditional arguments for atheism. Essential to the underlying assumptions of those arguments was the belief that people were capable of being rational agents able to make moral decisions and act upon them. For thinkers such as Feuerbach and Marx, God was simply a comforting illusion that, in order for humanity to advance, must be discarded. The notion of God restricted autonomy by making humanity dependent on

---

4. M. Riddell, *Threshold of the Future* (Great Britain: SPCK, 1998), 112.

an external authority that constricted our moral and intellectual development. If the idea of God could be done away with, then the autonomous modern self could be truly free to pursue its own destiny. It was Nietzsche who first called us to think through the implications of what the death of God really means for humanity. The only values available to us are those we construct ourselves, and therefore my values can have no greater claim than your values. If the notion of the modern self has collapsed, then there is no rational moral agent capable of finding truth, as illusory beliefs are all that there can be. The collapse of the modern self, for Nietzsche, has in fact meant the collapse of reason, hope and freedom.

The change in the concept of the self from the modern to the postmodern has a significant implication for Christian ministry that has not yet fully filtered through. Most Christians are well aware of the postmodern rejection of the notion of absolute truth. The main thrust of the Christian response to postmodernity thus far seems to have been to try to shore up the notion of objective truth to prevent it from collapsing into the subjective abyss of relativism. This may well be a useful project, but the problem is that the postmodern person is not really interested in the outcome. For the postmodern self, notions of truth, objective or otherwise, are no longer on the agenda. The real issue for them lies with the abuse of power. Shoring up the notion of objective truth is simply providing an answer to a question that people are no longer interested in asking.

For evangelical Christians this is a significant challenge. Part of the main selling point of the gospel message has been its claim to be the truth. This claim may well still be valid, but it no longer carries any weight with its intended audience, even if it can be proved. We have failed to grasp why the notion of truth is no longer an issue for the postmodern person, and so have therefore conveniently felt ourselves immune from the postmodern critique. The challenge of postmodernism for us in the church is particularly acute, as we are very vulnerable to a critique based upon an analysis of claims of power. We have been sucked into playing the modernist game of being obsessed with power – hook, line, and sinker.

The Christian response

In seeking to translate the gospel within the emerging postmodern condition, we stand in the long tradition of the historic Christian church working to speak the gospel in relevant terms to a new generation. The process of translation holds the promise not only that this generation will come to understand the gospel and therefore experience profound transformation in their thinking but also that the church will grow in its understanding of the gospel it seeks to proclaim.[5]

The obvious question raised by all this is: 'How should we as Christians respond to this shift in how the self is understood?' Can the message of the gospel still be relevant when questions of truth are no longer on the agenda?

What is clear is that our approach and methods need to change dramatically, given the shift in the concept of the self. The postmodern self is asking a different set of questions than the modern self was asking. If part of the task of conveying the message of the gospel is to provide 'answers', then we must ensure that we are responding to the questions that are actually being asked, rather than the ones we think are being asked.

We need a theology of hope to counter the prevailing postmodern message of despair

One real point of departure for Christians from the postmodern worldview is the differing underlying attitude. The postmodern framework provides a cynical, negative account of the world and our role and place in it, while the Christian framework can offer real hope and meaning. We should commend the more honest assessment of the state of the self and the world offered by postmodernism, but we would want to insist that this is not the complete picture. The self and the world is created by a God who loves and cares for all his creation. This is a real challenge for Christianity as it faces the daunting task of attempting to foster hope and trust, which is going against the postmodern flow of cynicism and suspicion. The Christian worldview attempts to chart a difficult middle path. It wants to reject the modernist assumption that everything can be known and subsequently controlled, but it also wants to reject the postmodern assumption that no meaning and purpose is possible.

---

5. G.R. Hunsenberger and C. Van Gelder (Eds) *The Church Between Gospel and Culture* (Grand Rapids: Eerdmans, 1996), 138.

Christianity can provide a centre for the self through being loved by God and the community of the church

The postmodern self finds itself the victim of two types of competing forces that want to shape and control it. Firstly there are the external forces of power claims and manipulative interests, and secondly there are the internal forces of a person's own drives and desires.

The Christian worldview once again wants to affirm the more honest analysis the postmodern perspective offers, that the self is subject to forces beyond its control. But the Christian would also want to affirm that a centre for the self is possible through being in a loving relationship with the creator God. With this relationship, the self can move beyond simply being tossed around by competing power interests and can start to shape its own life and identity. The self can have an anchor that can provide stability, hope and meaning by being reconstituted in the light of Christ's saving actions.

The Christian message argues that through the work of the Holy Spirit we can be transformed to be like Christ. This transformation helps lift the self out of its feeling of helplessness, and offers real hope for the future. This faith in Christ can turn the tide of cynicism and distrust. Self-interest and a desire to control and manipulate can be transformed into love for others.

The Christian framework of hope also enables people to have the courage to learn to accept themselves for who they really are. If there is a God who loves them, then they can learn to accept themselves and need no longer hide behind self-deceit. It is only in the context of a loving relationship with God and with others that the self can gain the confidence to discard its mask, and foster the caring environment which allows its real identity to emerge.

We need to provide an understanding of the story of the individual postmodern self as part of the larger narrative of God's saving actions in the world

Part of the Christian message in the postmodern age will be to help locate the individual postmodern self as part of the larger narrative of God's work in the world. Locating the individual's story as part of a larger story can provide real meaning and stability. The Christian narrative not only incorporates what has gone before, but it stretches out into the future, inviting the self to be a part of a larger story of hope and meaning for itself and for the world. 'The identity of the real self emerges fully only in relation to purposes which transcend the self.'[6]

We need to help free the postmodern self from the chains that hold it captive

If we are serious about freeing the postmodern person from bondage to the world, then we need to be prepared to name and challenge the things that bind. We need to be prepared to challenge those in society who hold power, and speak for those whom the system renders powerless. An important task of pre-evangelism will be to name the things that hold the self captive, and to speak for those who have no voice.

The implications for youth ministry

We need to take the challenge offered by postmodernism seriously

As a group of people called to minister to young people, we need to be at the forefront of engagement with postmodernity and thinking through its implications for Christian ministry. We need to avoid getting sidetracked into unhelpful philosophical debates about the nature of truth. Instead we need to acknowledge the force of the postmodern critique for Christianity. The postmodern paradigm shift is an invitation for us to honestly assess how we go about ministry, and the role power plays in it. 'We are not speaking of some esoteric epistemological debate which is awaiting Christian approval to proceed, but of the shape of the emerging context for which Christian mission must take place.'[7]

Unlike some attitudes prevalent in the literature on Christian engagement with postmodernism, we are not at some sort of cultural buffet where we can select the best bits of the postmodern worldview and reject the bits we don't like. For the postmodern person the medium is the message, and we cannot escape the harsh reality that our medium is seen as an irrelevant modern institution.

Youth ministry will feel acutely the challenge to be relevant to the postmodern self, as we are part of a church that is caught in the tension

---

6. Thiselton, 76.
7. Riddell, 102.

between trying to be in both mission and survival modes at the same time.

> A missionary church needs to be open, flexible, reflective, experimental, dynamic and energetic. In order to survive in difficult times, on the other hand, a church will adopt practices which are conservative, exclusive, orthodox, static, careful, and scrupulous. This is how institutions survive. Unfortunately, it is also how movements die.[8]

We need to develop new ministry and theological frameworks that cater to the postmodern rather than to the modern self

Most of our models of ministry arose in order to respond to the needs of the modern self, and they need to be significantly modified in their emphases in order to be relevant to the postmodern conception of the self.

For example, many of our theological frameworks are constructed with modernist assumptions in mind. Our doctrines of salvation have an individualistic flavour emphasising the importance of the 'vertical' relationship between the individual and God, while ignoring the 'horizontal' relationships between the person and their community, and the world in which they live. Sin is often reduced to the stuff that prevents us from achieving our own individual autonomy and freedom. Salvation has become an individualistic matter of whether you are in a right legal status before God the great cosmic judge.

The postmodern self has much more of an understanding of the notion of a fallen humanity. It does not take much to convince people that the world is stuffed. We need to develop more community models of redemption that emphasise how Christ's saving actions redeemed the whole of humanity and creation, rather than someone who died for me as an individual. We need to emphasise Jesus as the Suffering Servant whose love for humanity was profoundly demonstrated by his sacrificial death on the cross. The new life that is made possible through his resurrection is the ultimate free gift available to the whole of creation. Atonement models that are based around legal transactional metaphors or that over-emphasise judgment will not be as warmly received by the postmodern self, as they are more susceptible to being misused for manipulative ends by those in authority.

---

8. Riddell, 13.

Another challenge for the gospel message in this postmodern age is to encourage the postmodern self to accept responsibility for its own actions. We need to reject the postmodern tendency to blame one's plight on external factors, and encourage a person to acknowledge his/her own part in the brokenness of the world. Yes they are victims, but they also play their part as victimisers. To be truly a part of the solution, they must be encouraged to acknowledge their own part in the problem.

We need a new paradigm of Christian leadership based on the self-giving of Christ

The heart of the Christian message is the Cross of Christ, which provides the ultimate example of God's self-giving love. We must be serious about modelling our lives on Jesus, whose life and death is the greatest example of non-manipulative love the world has ever known. The new paradigm for Christian leadership for our postmodern times is based on the idea of the 'gift', and finds its expression in acts of self-giving service to others. The model involves leaders giving freely of themselves, motivated not by their own self interest but instead by love for others. The model of the gift is not new of course, as it derives from the example of Jesus and is found in his teaching when he declares in Matthew 23:11: 'The greatest among you will be your servant.' One of the real turn-off factors for postmodern people is individuals and groups using power for manipulative ends. Postmodernism says people want to lead to fulfil their own need for power and domination. The model of the gift defuses this critique by asking for nothing in return.

While most of us in the church would be well-versed in the rhetoric of the servant leader as the model for Christian leadership, more often than not our practices fail to translate these words into action. As the church moved from being at the centre of all aspects of life in the Middle Ages to being on the periphery of society in our postmodern times, it has dealt with this increasing marginalisation by attempting to become more corporate and professional in order to hang onto its last vestiges of status and respect in the community.

> The pastors have metamorphosed into a company of shopkeepers, and the shops they keep are churches. They are preoccupied with shopkeepers concerns – how to keep the customers happy, how to lure customers away

from competitors down the street, how to package the goods so the customer will lay out more money.[9]

We, in the church, have been quick to adopt secular leadership strategies and to model our ministries based on corporate examples. I don't want to suggest that there are not useful insights to be gained from these models, but we need to be careful of the subtle influence of their underlying philosophy. The ultimate benefit of these strategies is not intended to be the empowerment of others, but increasing the power of the individual.

Secular leadership models will never understand or be able to capture adequately the seemingly contradictory message at the centre of the gospel, that in order to gain your life you must lose it. Paul was familiar with a model of religious leadership that the secular world found difficult to comprehend. In 1 Corinthians he mocks the church at Corinth for being obsessed with secular leadership traits, such as being a skilled orator. True discipleship for Paul depends on identification with Christ, who did not seek power by manipulative means or for his own status. This is a message that runs fundamentally counter to the ethos of secular models of leadership. We need to rediscover a genuine model of servant leadership which does not simply copy the corporate hierarchical structure, but truly exhibits a humble 'servant' attitude. If we continue to be obsessed by secular leadership strategies, then we run the real risk of alienating the postmodern self from the kingdom of God.

We need to end the divisive factional politics in the church

Political factionalism within the church is running rampant towards the end of the millennium. In the Anglican Church we have a polarised two-party system, with a growing group occupying the middle ground who are uncomfortable with the extremes of both factions and feel increasingly isolated and disenfranchised. For a group that is allegedly interested in the truth, there are few if any constructive forums available to discuss the important issues within the church. Instead we have factionalism pure and simple that can easily compete with the worst of Canberra's political machinations. This obsession with political manoeuvring runs the major risk of alienating young people from the church. We should be attempting to provide alternative, less

---

9. Peterson quoted in Riddell, 176.

divisive models, rather than working on perfecting the more Machiavellian aspects of our church politics. For the young, these political groups may well say they are concerned with doing God's will, but this defence collapses under closer scrutiny as it becomes clear that the priority is political power.

We need diverse ministries and a framework that enables these differing ministries to be respected

Most books and articles about postmodernism are quick to mention how diverse the postmodern generation is. While this diversity is readily acknowledged in the literature, it has not yet filtered down to how we go about doing Christian ministry. We have yet to make the simple step of realising that a diversity of ministry options is essential to reaching this generation. We still tend to have the one framework for evangelism, or the one discipleship strategy, and we find it very difficult to value and respect ministries which differ from our own.

We are generally pretty parochial about our own church and what we are doing. We easily fall into the trap of thinking that we at St Cuthbert's have *the strategy* or *the program*, and if you are not doing something similar then you cannot be serious about wanting to extend the kingdom of God. There is a tendency to universalise what works for us in our particular situation, and to say that is what the rest of the church should be doing. But if the church as a whole pursues the one strategy, we will not adequately cater to the postmodern self, which needs diversity and variety in order to be reached.

It is important therefore to provide constructive forums where different ministry models can be shared and learned from. We also need an attitude of respect for those engaged in Christian ministry who do things differently from us. If someone is not comfortable with the high powered all singing and dancing youth service that occurs where we work at St Nathan's, are we really willing to recommend a more appropriate service for him/her, which might be the more reflective service taking place down the road at St Philmore's?

Another unfortunate consequence of divisive factionalism rampant in the church is that certain forms of ministry have become politicised. If you identify with one sort of group in the church then you are expected to run certain types of ministry. Alpha courses for example are used in some churches which are slightly more 'touchy-feely', and those with so-called Bible-centred teaching frown upon certain elements. If you identify yourself as an evangelical church, then you would not dream of running a Taize style service as that is perceived to be aligned with another church grouping.

It is no longer adequate to be running our styles of ministry based on political considerations, rather than on meeting the need of the people. It is time for pragmatism to become the new overriding strategy rather than politics. If a certain type or style of ministry works in terms of helping the postmodern self move closer to God, then surely that should be the overriding concern. It is now a well-established fact that, for young people, denominational boundaries are rapidly losing their significance. I believe the same is true of churchmanship boundaries. What is important for young people is whether a form of worship works for them, rather than which factional group endorses it.

Multiple models of ministry and theology are important, not just to ensure that we cater adequately to a diverse postmodern generation, but also as a vital part the system of checks and balances that ensure we do not abuse or distort our power. Problems of abuse and manipulation tend to arise when one model is used in isolation, or over-emphasised.

We need to share our resources, try each other's styles, break down the divisions and get back to what we are supposed to be on about, which is reaching people with the message of the gospel.

Chapter Six

Worship, community and the triune God of Grace

Olivia Moffatt

What is worship?

It seems that everybody does it.

Sooner or later it slips out even if you are aware that it's not correct. Just as the congregation is about to sing, you say, 'Let's really worship God now!' Or perhaps your Sunday gatherings are called *worship services*? Or the group which organises those services is called the *worship team*? On the other hand, I've never heard anyone describe their Monday to Friday job as worship, nor is it a word used by the volunteer at our Church when she is mopping the hall floor, and it definitely never comes out of my mouth after a service which has been too long or boring.

Unfortunately it's not just at the popular level that the word has come to mean 'what we do when we gather together as Christians on Sunday'. Willamon has written an important book called *Worship as Pastoral Care* because he wants to encourage us to use our Sunday services as an opportunity to give and receive some real pastoral care.[1] He assumes from start to finish that 'worship' is about our Sunday services. Robert Webber makes the same mistake in *Worship is a Verb*. He wants the congregation to do more than warm a pew during a Sunday service – an admirable goal. But again it's a very limiting use of the word worship.[2] Professor Geoffrey Wainwright has written a systematic theology from the viewpoint of worship in which he describes it as 'the point of concentration at which the whole of the

---

1. W.H. Willamon, *Worship as Pastoral Care* (Nashville: Abingdon Press, 1979).
2. R.E. Webber, *Worship is a verb* (Waco: Word, 1987).

Christian life comes to ritual focus'.³ Again our Sunday gatherings are on view. Tom Wright in his excellent little book *For All God's Worth* uses another popular definition.

Etymologically worship derives from 'worth-ship', and thus means to give God all his worth.⁴ We are to live all of our lives in a way which signifies and responds to God's worth. This is a much better definition than Sunday services, since it encompasses all of life. (This is a point the New Testament strongly affirms, as we shall see.) However even this picture of 'worship' makes the mistake of using the definition of an English word, when all along that word has been a less than adequate translation for a range of Hebrew and Greek words. Wright's definition is so broad as to be practically useless. We need to ask further questions. What is God worth? What does giving this 'worth' look like? How do we do it? When? Where? With whom? And so on. Fortunately an investigation into the original meaning of the words will serve us well in painting some detail onto Wright's broad canvas.

What does the Old Testament mean by worship?

There are a number of Hebrew words which we translate as worship.⁵ It is clear that there is a development in complexity as Israel responds to the ever deepening revelation from YHWH, but patterns and places do emerge. I will briefly focus on: adoration, service, priesthood, sacrifice, the law and covenant.

First of all the Old Testament uses a series of words to express acts of adoration, prostration, praise and thanksgiving. One in particular, *histahawah*, occurs frequently and means to bow down and prostrate one's self. This was a common act in the Ancient Near East before both earthly rulers and gods. An attitude of worshipful reverence belongs with this external act. It was an act of homage, which was fundamentally about submission. To describe praising God there are two main words: *barah* 'to bless' and *yadah* ' to put forth'.⁶ Today when we repent, when we are submitting ourselves (again) to the Lordship of

---

3. G. Wainwright, *Doxology, A Systematic Theology, The praise of God in Worship, Doctrine and Life* (London: Epworth Press, 1980), 8.
4. T. Wright, *For All God's Worth* (London: Triangle, 1997), 1.
5. For an excellent and concise overview see Y. Hattori, 'Theology of Worship in the Old Testament', *Worship: Adoration and Action*, editor D.A. Carson, (Carlisle: The Paternoster Press, 1993), 21–50.
6. Hattori, 23–24.

Christ we are engaging in *histahawah*. This can involve being moved to raise our hands, bow our heads, or fall to our knees in worship thus visibly expressing the awe, wonder and adoration that these words point to, as long as we are actually submitting our hearts and lives to God at the same time.

The other common Old Testament term is *abad*, which means 'to serve'. Again in Hebrew it was used in religious and non-religious contexts. One could serve a heavenly or earthly master. The nature of the service rendered to God altered through the times of the tabernacle, temple and exile, as did those who were considered fit to perform the service. However, for most of Israel's history, the priests performed the acceptable cultic acts of service to which *abad* most often refers. The word for priestly service in the LXX is *leitourgein*, and it is only used of priests serving the nation Israel and for Levites who serve the priests.

The third area to focus on briefly is that of sacrifice. Like the concepts above, great volumes could be written and have been written on sacrifice alone. Yet in my tradition (evangelicalism) at a popular level, it seems to be largely misunderstood. The assumption often is that all the Old Testament sacrifices were both substitutional and atoning and thus all point to Christ's work on the Cross, end of story. Therefore any use of the word today implies atonement, and since only Christ can effectively atone for sins, 'sacrifice' has become a word to avoid using. However we run into problems when we read Paul who wrote 'even if I am being poured out as a libation over the sacrifice and the offering of your faith, I am glad and rejoice with all of you' (Philippians 2:17). I remember as a young Christian asking my minister about this because I was worried that Paul was implying that the offering of his life in service and suffering somehow made the Philippians' faith more acceptable to God. Fortunately the many Hebrew words used for sacrifice describe a broad and helpful picture. Most importantly, there *are* sin offerings *(hattath)* and guilt offerings *(asham)* as well as the Passover and the Day of Atonement. Further 'whoever acts high-handedly ... shall be utterly cut off and bear the guilt' (Numbers 15:30–31). That is, the above sin offerings and mechanisms are for unintentional sins! But of course, Old Testament sacrifices also included offerings of dedication and thanksgiving (*olah* – whole burnt offerings), gift offerings, especially first-fruits (*minhah* – cereal or meat offering), and peace offerings (*shelamin*).⁷ Delight in God naturally led to the regular and wholehearted offering of these sacrifices to him. It was a way to honour God in all of life, giving back the best of what God had given.

Any mention of honouring God in all aspects of life brings up the topic of the Law in the Old Testament. Again a vast and hotly debated subject! It is probably sufficient for this paper to describe the law as the God-given requirements for a worshipping community. One scholar describes the Old Testament law as embodying the spirit of *abad* (service) and laying the foundation for the cultic expression of that service.⁸ The eighth century prophets certainly share that understanding, and remind Israel that cultic *abad* merely heaps judgment upon them if it is not accompanied by heartfelt obedience to the law.⁹ Finally the focus on the giving of the law in Exodus makes 'word-oriented' worship central, as the law is recited, taught by priests and parents, learned and lived out.¹⁰

Looking at sacrifice and law introduces the idea of acceptable worship. God reveals himself to us and in so doing establishes the means by which any person can be in relationship with him and his people. God reveals himself, God reveals how we are to relate to him and God provides the means to do it. Therefore it is very important to explicitly discuss what I believe is the unifying theme of the Old Testament: covenant (*berit*). A covenant is a binding alliance or treaty between two or more parties, often where one party is manifestly superior. In the latter case, a king, for example, promises protection to a people who offer loyalty and service. As such the concept was a familiar one in the Ancient Near East. The covenants that God makes with Noah, Abram, Israel at Sinai, and David, bind God to the people and the people to God. The details of the covenant express who God is and what is acceptable to him and what he is offering to those who covenant with him. Acceptable adoration, service, sacrifice and living out of the law are details of the covenant. Importantly God chose a people and invited

---

7. For a comprehensive introduction to the variety and meaning of Old Testament sacrifices see: R.T. Beckwith, 'Sacrifice and Offering', *New Bible Dictionary*, eds J.D. Douglas, N. Hillyer, F.F. Bruce, D. Guthrie, A.R. Millard, J.I. Packer, D.J. Wiseman, (Leicester: Inter-Varsity Press, 1962 (1982)), 1045–1054.
8. Hattori, 28–29.
9. One example is Isaiah 1:12–17.
10. Hattori, 29.

them into a covenant. He did not select for himself those who were living according to the requirements of his covenant. It has always been about grace.

In summary it is clear that Old Testament worship involved specific cultic acts of service as well as heartfelt adoration and praise. Furthermore the giving of the law within the framework of the covenant ensured acceptable worship in everyday life.

What does the New Testament mean by worship?

In Christ we see the fulfilment of so much of the Old Testament. So Christ alters our understanding and practice of worship by his own actions. What is not grounded and fulfilled in him, is altered by being reflected through him, like light through a prism. Now we see many more colours and dimensions than before, although we recognise the similarities and acknowledge that the source of our concepts is the Old Testament.

By examining the LXX, we can start to understand the continuity of some ideas from Old to New. The Hebrew term *histahawah* was translated by *proskynein*. This term is mostly used in the New Testament of people's response to Jesus, during both his earthly life (for example Matthew 14:33; John 9:38) and his ascended reign (Revelation 4:10).[11] *Abad* was translated by the Greek *latreuein*. Through its prominence in the LXX it came to refer exclusively to service rendered to God or the pagan gods. The New Testament uses *latreuein* to refer to Israel's cultic practices but also, and most importantly, the terminology is used to refer to the new way of relating to God made possible through Jesus Christ (for example Romans 12:1; Philippians 3:3; Hebrews 9:14).[12]

Thus we see that, in the New Testament, worship is still about adoration and action.

Deeper understanding of the meaning of worship for Christians is only possible after we look at Jesus: perfect worshipper, perfect priest and perfect sacrifice. Jesus is the only obedient and perfect worshipper. In his rebuttal to Satan during the temptation in the wilderness, Jesus asserts that he will only worship *(proskyneseis)* God and serve *(latreuseis)*

---

11. D. Peterson, 'Worship in the New Testament', *Worship: Adoration and Action*, 52.
12. Peterson, 54.

him alone (for example Luke 4:5–8). This obedience takes Jesus all the way to the Cross. The Cross is the place where Jesus offers the perfect sacrifice of himself on behalf of sinners. He tells his disciples that his life is a ransom which will buy back many (Mark 10:45). This implies a substitution. The setting of the Passover and Jesus' teaching in his new words during the meal add further to this picture. Especially the cup-words of 'my blood of the covenant' (Mark 14:24) show Jesus as the definitive sacrifice by which a new and enduring covenant between God and all the peoples of the earth would be established.[13] Paul uses the ideas of sacrifice many times when discussing Christ's death. In Ephesians 5:2, Jesus is 'a fragrant offering and sacrifice to God'. Romans 3:25 states that Jesus was put forward by God 'as a sacrifice of atonement by his blood.' These and other references lead one scholar to conclude that for Paul, Jesus has fulfilled the Day of Atonement sin offering and rendered the whole Old Testament sacrificial system unnecessary.[14]

The writer of the book of Hebrews develops much more fully both the idea of Jesus as perfect worshipper and perfect sacrifice. Further, only Hebrews identifies Jesus as the perfect priest – the great High Priest, although there are other New Testament allusions to Jesus in that role (for example Romans 8:34; 1 John 2:1–2). In Hebrews, the teaching about Jesus as the perfect and obedient worshipper, even unto death, occurs in at least three places: Hebrews 5:7–9, 7:27, 9:14. He is the perfect and unblemished sacrifice (7:27, 9:14), which is a unique, once for all, sacrifice (7:27, 9:24–28, 10:10–14), and which institutes a new covenant that sets aside the old (8:13, 9:1–10, 10:9–14). Further Christ does all this as our great high priest. He is our worship leader *(leitourgas)*. The sacrifice and priest are one, and now he lives to intercede for us and continue in his priestly role leading us in our worship (5:6, 10, 6:20, 7:1–28). The Old Testament system was a copy of the eternal heavenly reality in which Christ ministers (9:23–24). Although focused on Christ this is a profoundly Trinitarian picture. We are 'in Christ' by the Holy Spirit. Before the throne of the Father, we join our worship to Christ's as he leads us in that worship.[15]

---

13. Peterson, 56–61.
14. Peterson, 58–59.
15. J. Torrance, *Worship, Community and the Triune God of Grace* (Carlisle: Paternoster Press, 1996), 32–56.

It is clear then that compared to the old covenant, the new is very familiar in terms and concepts and yet radically different. So how do Christians offer acceptable worship today? The short answer is 'in Christ'. Paul often began his letters with a greeting which described the recipients as his brethren or saints 'in Christ' (for example Colossians 1:2, Philippians 1:1). This profound, exciting and awe inspiring idea is perhaps one which we take for granted, losing its impact. By faith we are not only in God's family, we are also 'in Christ'. In Colossians 2:6 Paul exhorts the readers ' As you therefore have received Christ Jesus the Lord, continue to live your lives in him'. He is the head of the Church which is his body (Ephesians 4:15-16; 1 Corinthians 12:13, 27). It is not possible to have a more intimate relationship with God. There is no further access possible, no place where we cannot go, no other mediator required – **ever**. I think that for Paul, being 'in Christ' was the centre of his theology. When the Father loves his own Son, he is loving us. When we worship the Father we do so intimately through being in Christ. We are part of God *ad intra*.

There are a number of ways in which this theme of being 'in Christ' is developed. Jesus himself knew that as the Son of God present in Israel's midst, he was greater than the Temple (Matthew 12:6). Therefore worshipping at the Temple, where God located himself, was no longer necessary when God was located in Christ walking around. In this and other ways the Gospels indicate that Jesus himself is to become the centre of salvation and blessing for all Israel and the nations.[16] In Matthew 18:20, Jesus promises to be present when people gather in his name to pray. Jesus represents God's royal presence and authority more fully than even the Temple. Therefore he can say to the Samaritan woman in John 4 that in reality the place of worship will no longer matter. The Jews were right, but even their way of worship is to be superseded. God seeks worshippers who worship in Spirit and truth (*proskynein* used throughout). John 3 has already shown us that God, the Father, begets true worshippers through the Spirit. John 7:37-39 goes on to teach us that Jesus makes the Spirit available to those who come to him, based on his saving work. In this fantastic Trinitarian picture of new worship from John, we see that Jesus is the means of entering into true worship.[17]

---

16. Peterson, 61–63.
17. Peterson, 63–64.

Jesus is the vehicle for us to come before the Father, but he is much more than that. He is also the object of our worship. The New Testament writers clearly claim divine honour belongs to Jesus. In the Gospels various supplicants come and bow before him *(proskynein)* (for example Matthew 8:2, 9:18). When Jesus walked on water to the disciples rowing against the wind, their response was to proclaim him the Son of God and to worship *(proskynein)* him (Matthew 14:33). Paul ascribes divine honour to Jesus when he reminds the Romans in 10:8–13 that all who confess Jesus as Lord will be saved. He goes on to quote Joel 2:32: 'everyone who calls on the name of the Lord shall be saved'. Joel clearly meant YHWH, the one true God. Paul ascribes this Lordship, and thus divinity, to Jesus. Peter effectively does the same thing in his first sermon on the day of Pentecost (Acts 2, especially verse 36).

The New Testament is very clear that this new way of worshipping God encompasses all our lives. In Romans 12:1-3, Paul uses the language of worship and sacrifice to urge the readers to offer up their bodies (that is their lives, all of themselves). He describes this worship as their *'logike latreia'*, literally their reasonable or intelligent service. Further, the way to do this is to be transformed through the renewing of their minds, rather than conforming to the spirit of the age. It's very important to see that this is a 'word-oriented' form of worship, in the sense that we are to offer up all of ourselves to God as a response of understanding to the gospel. It means to live a life which is consonant with the truths of the gospel. Further transformation begins with the mind, so we need to be taught and to read and reflect on the gospel and the Bible. Paul himself gives a direct example of what living worship looks like. In Chapter 14 of Romans he applies the gospel to the weak and strong in the congregation in Rome. The strong are to put no stumbling block in the way of the weak over the eating of certain foods. In verse 18 he says, 'the one who thus serves Christ is acceptable to God and has human approval'.[18]

Equally it can be shown that the writer to the Hebrews and other New Testament writers explicitly draw out implications for worshipping in and through our everyday lives as a response to understanding Christ's atoning sacrifice.[19] This is very important when we consider

---

18. Peterson, 68–69.
19. Peterson, 73–74.

implications of Old Testament law, and its fulfilment in Christ and living by the Spirit. It is a huge and controversial area of theological discussion. However the New Testament clearly presents the fact that all of life is surrendered to God in obedient worship, not merely obedience to the law (however you resolve those ideas!). The Greek for priestly service in the LXX is, as mentioned, *leitourgein*. In the New Testament, priestly service can be about evangelism, see below, but mainly focuses on serving one another in all of life. All believers can perform priestly service in their everyday worship of God. See for example 2 Corinthians 9:12; Philippians 2:25, 30.

One more dimension of the transformation of the Old Testament ideas in the New Testament needs to be mentioned. Paul describes his apostolic and evangelistic ministry as 'the priestly service of the gospel of God, so that the offering of the Gentiles may be acceptable, sanctified by the Holy Spirit' (Romans 15:16). This is the only time he refers to himself in such cultic terms, and note its focus: evangelism! He uses a related word, which in Old Testament usage inferred cultic service, later in the same chapter when he describes the Gentile Churches financial support to the Christians in Jerusalem.(Romans 15:27; also 2 Corinthians 9:12). The transformation of worship language is complete. We worship and serve God in the world through evangelism, and by practical material sharing in our everyday lives as we live out and proclaim that gospel.

At this stage it is appropriate to give a definition of worship. Peterson, whose outline I have been using above, describes worship as 'our engagement with God through faith in Jesus Christ and what he has done for us.'[20] I would add to this definition that it is our engagement with God as Father, Son and Holy Spirit. We submit and pay homage to the three Persons of the Trinity. We also engage with the Father, through faith in Jesus and by his work, empowered by the Holy Spirit. As I show from James Torrance's work below, it is important to engage with God through Christ, but not to focus so exclusively on Christ that the Trinity is effectively hidden. However it is ever true that Christ is the integrating reality of Trinitarian theology.[21] Further, our

---

20. Peterson, 52.
21. P. Hoon, *The Integrity of Worship* (Nashville: Abingdon Press, 1971), 115, quoted in J. Thompson, *Modern Trinitarian Perspectives* (Oxford: Oxford University Press, 1994), 95.

engagement with this Trinitarian God happens in every area of our life, as we live distinctively and in holiness (set apart in our living). Therefore throughout this paper I have endeavoured to use worship to refer to all of life. Our gatherings *(ekklesia)* are also worship, but they do not exhaust the meaning of that word, rather they focus and facilitate our everyday living. We often think that our time of gathering is when we focus more on God than at other times of the week. I would argue that if there is any major emphasis to our gatherings it is edification. This emphasis is clear in both Paul and Hebrews. See 1 Corinthians 14, 1 Thessalonians 5:11, Ephesians 4:11-16 and Hebrews 10 for examples of this prevalent teaching.[22]

Three theological models and their impact on our (Sunday) gatherings

The following three models have been proposed by James Torrance, a Scottish Reformed Presbyterian. He is a lecturer at the University of Aberdeen, and at Fuller Seminary. He has taught the Master class at Ridley College, which is where I first heard him speak. The models have been published in various reports, journals and books and can be found in his recent book *Worship, Community and the Triune God of Grace*.[23]

Model 1: the Harnack (Hick) model

This is the model of nineteenth century Protestant liberalism given classical expression by Adolf Harnack, recently revived and modified by John Hick. According to this, the heart of religion is the soul's immediate relationship to God. The Bible gives us many examples of people relating to God, of which the Father-Son relationship between Jesus and God is the most important. We worship God, revealed as Father, but not Jesus, nor the Spirit. In Harnack's own words, 'The Gospel, as Jesus proclaimed it, has to do with the Father only and not with the Son.'[24] Nothing must come between the soul's relationship with God the Father, be it sacrifices, priests, covenant law, doctrine, or Jesus Christ himself! This view is clearly unitarian and individualistic.

---

22. Peterson, 71-95.
23. See also *The Forgotten Trinity: The Report of the B.C.C. Study Commission on Trinitarian Doctrine Today* (London: InterChurch House, 3 vols, 1989) and J. Torrance, *Theology of Ministry and Worship* (Melbourne: Fuller Theological Seminary, 1993).
24. A. Harnack *What is Christianity?* (New York: Harper, 1957), 144.

The centre of everything is our immediate relationship with God, our present-day experience. The Father-Son relationship is generic not unique. In the end this view denies grace and thus becomes moralistic.[25] As soon as the question is asked, 'How do we relate to God?', either our sin or God's holy otherness must be denied. This view, in its claim to free us and make God a God of love, actually limits and denies whole areas of God's being and our reality. Therefore it is imperative that when we gather we must not sing, pray, communion or preach as though we imitate *directly* (and from our own ability) the intimacy of the Father-Son relationship.

Model 2: the existential, experience model

This model has a number of permutations and can be seen reflected in some liberal churches as well as some evangelical and charismatic churches. Its centre is 'God and me today'. The focus is on God's present grace, to which we respond in repentance, faith and decision. Although the centre is the present moment, a response of faith is only made possible by the work of Christ on the Cross. Thus the event of the Cross, through the event of preaching, gives rise to the event of faith. This can be interpreted in radical existential terms, as in Bultmann, or in more evangelical terms as in the early Barth.[26]

This model is so familiar to many of us in terms of what we actually do on a Sunday together that we wonder what is wrong with it. According to Torrance, the event-oriented nature of each Sunday stresses the work of Christ at the expense of His person. Thus, the gospel is about 'events', with little or no ontology. We become a people for whom the centre of religious experience is grace, rather than Christ. As Bonhoeffer commented, we become more interested in the blessings of Christ than Christ himself. The most serious problem though is failing to recognise that salvation is not simply through the work of Christ, but primarily given to us in his person. We are 'in Christ'.

Ironically, in seeking to focus on grace, people who gather from week to week based on this 'event' model actually undermine the full grace which God showers on us. We draw near to God in and through Christ in the communion of the Spirit. We do not stand alone and individually before God because Christ's work, grasped by faith, has

---

25. Torrance, 12–13.
26. Torrance, 13–18.

made us clean. No! We stand before God 'in Christ', the only pure one. Thus, this model is too human-centred in emphasising our decision, our faith, our repentance. It acknowledges that Jesus provides the means, but then throws us back upon ourselves in our response. It has no understanding of Christ as our continuing great high priest. He is our *leitourgos* now! It is he who leads our worship, bears our sorrows and intercedes for us, presenting us to the Father as his dear children and uniting us with himself by the Holy Spirit. Whatever else faith is, it is a response to the Response already being made for us and continually being made for us in Christ, the pioneer of our faith.

Model 3: Torrance's Trinitarian model

The starting point here is with the eternally triune God, stressing that worship is the gift of participating through the Spirit in the incarnate Son's communion with the Father. At the centre stands the unique relationship between the Father and the Son, who dwell in the unity and communion of the Spirit. Jesus presents himself in our humanity through the eternal spirit to the Father on behalf of humankind. We participate by being in Christ by the Holy Spirit. Moreover we are Christ's body, the Church, joined to him by the Spirit, a corporate image which is central in the New Testament. Further our communion in Christ means we are all members of the one body and as such we relate to each other in the Spirit. All these relationships reflect God in his innermost being. What God is in his innermost being, he is towards us. We relate to God not in the same way that Jesus did (as per Harnack) but by gracious invitation to participate in the unique Father-Son relationship by the Spirit.[27]

Putting flesh on the Trinitarian model

Apart from the great strengths mentioned above, and the primary intention that only the Trinitarian model faithfully represents both biblical and systematic truth about God, we still need to know more of what this kind of worship looks like. Torrance presents a fairly academic picture, although he does explicitly discuss both Baptism and Communion.

Baptism is baptism into the one baptism of Christ. By the Spirit we participate in the vicarious baptism of Christ. The gospel is that Christ

---

27. Torrance, 18–22.

was baptised in blood on the Cross, once and for all, one for all.[28] In this way his death was our death, his burial our burial, his resurrection, our resurrection. The baptismal liturgy of the French Reformed Church expresses vividly the substitutionary nature of Christ's actions for us and our participation in them and in Christ by the act of baptism: 'Little child, for you Jesus Christ has come, he has fought, he has suffered. For you he entered the shadow of Gethsemane and the horror of Calvary. For you he uttered the cry "It is finished!" For you he rose from the dead and ascended into heaven and there he intercedes – for you little child, even though you don't know it. But in this way the word of the gospel becomes true. "We love him, because he first loved us." '[29] At baptism we remember that Christ was for us, before Christ was in us. Christ does not come to us because we were first for him! Thus baptism is a sign of what the triune God does: God forgives, God cleanses, God regenerates, God adopts, God sends the Spirit into our hearts so that we can cry 'Abba Father!' In baptising children of believers we stress the grace of God and the work of Christ. In baptising in water we stress the cleansing through Christ by the Spirit. When it is a full immersion baptism we stress the passive nature of being buried and coming back to life.

The Lord's Supper is an act of remembrance[30] and communion. The Christ we remember is not absent in communion, he is present by the Spirit to bring the things we celebrate to our remembrance in the act of communion. Christ always has a twofold ministry, the earthly and the heavenly. Through the Spirit he exercises these during communion by bringing to our remembrance the things of his once-for-all earthly ministry, and by lifting up our hearts and minds into his communion with the Father. On the one hand, Christ meets with us around his table, as the one in whose humanity our humanity was assumed and judged, the one in whose self-offering and self-consecration we were consecrated and healed. On the other hand, he is the ascended Lord in whose continuing humanity our humanity is presented by our Great High Priest to the Father. Thus in the words of Calvin, Christ is in a manner present and in a manner absent *(Quodammodo praesens et*

---

28. Jesus himself refers to his death on the cross as a baptism. See Luke 12:50.
29. Torrance, 65.
30. Remembrance is much more than recalling to mind events from the past and responding in gratitude. It is anamnesis, a concept which in the Bible is liturgically rich. It means remembering in such a way that we see our participation in the past event and see our destiny and future as bound up with that. See Torrance, 74–75.

quodammodo absens). The Holy Spirit exercises a twofold ministry which corresponds to the twofold ministry of Christ. Firstly the Spirit takes the things of Christ and ministers them to us by meeting us in communion worship, and summons us to respond with repentance, faith and an offering of ourselves as living sacrifices. Secondly the Spirit helps us in our frail and broken response, by lifting us up into Christ's ascended humanity, to be presented with Christ and the Spirit to the Father. The Spirit has a mediatorial role too, interceding with 'sighs too deep for words' (Romans 8:26).[31]

Non-sacramental models of Communion too easily throw us back on ourselves. They stress the involvement of God in the God-humanward movement but not in the human-Godward movement. That is left up to us as we recall the events of 2000 years ago in gratitude. Churches which gather according to Model 2 (the Existential, Experience model) often reflect what I would call a non-sacramental view, or at least a view which is much more limited and reduced than the one elucidated above. In so doing they are thrown back upon themselves to respond to Jesus' historical acts in and of themselves, to somehow be able to offer themselves as living sacrifices. This is to lose much of the comfort of the gospel. God throws us back onto **himself**, he helps our infirmities by giving us Jesus Christ and the Holy Spirit to make the appropriate response for us and in us. Communion profoundly expresses this as we feed on Christ and take the sacrament of his body and blood into our bodies.

Torrance does mention prayer in passing, as he discusses Christ as our *leitourgas*.[32] When we can't pray, when we don't know how to pray, Christ (and the Spirit) are praying for us. Our first pastoral response is to remind one another of this grace in which we stand. When we pray we add our prayers to those of our worship leader – our Great High Priest who stands before the throne of grace. Prayer is participation in the life of the Trinity.

A major limitation in Torrance's presentation is that he only explores the impact of this Trinitarian model on the use and expression of the sacraments and on prayer (in passing). We gather together for more than sacramental reasons. John Thompson points out that much

---

31. Torrance, 58–83.
32. Torrance, 32–57.

Trinitarian theology of worship focuses on prayer and sacraments but not on the word. However this was not true for the early Church. Their preaching was explicitly Trinitarian. The apostolic testimony is that the Jesus who was crucified 'God raised up ... being therefore exalted at the right hand of God, and having received from the Father the promise of the Holy Spirit, he has poured out this that you both see and hear' (Acts 2:32-33). From this apostolic kerygma the ancient Church wrestled basic Trinitarian concepts in dogmatic form. Yet as mentioned above Christ remained the integrating reality, the centrepiece. We see this particularly clearly when we turn to the place of the Bible in our gatherings. The Word of God is Christ, and yet we are able to also call the Scriptures the Word of God, analogous to the living Word by being both divine and human. The unity of Word and Spirit is central to our knowledge of the triune God. Through the written Word the Holy Spirit leads to the Living Word who is before the throne of the Father. Through the written Word, God by his Spirit is among us, encouraging us, challenging us, teaching us and transforming us. Again the twofold ministry of God – earthly and heavenly – is on view.

The preaching of the Bible is also affected by the way in which we understand our relationship to God. John Piper in a recent article clearly opposed what might be the common preaching outcome in churches which follow Model 2. While he extols much contemporary worship music as being directed God-ward, he finds that most preaching is very firmly human-centred. It's main purpose then is to help us live up to the Christian ideal by dealing with our current problems. It focuses on personal problems and relationships in a bid to be relevant and useful. Piper calls us back to what he calls preaching as 'expository exultation' – God exalting preaching. He states 'My aim ... is to plead for preaching to be pulled up – not away from the people's pain, but along with it into the presence of God, whose presence and reality alone is the final answer.'[33] Piper further states that this is God's own desire and he enables it to happen by his Holy Spirit. Very clearly this is preaching according to Model 3.

Finally I want to briefly examine the place of evangelism in our gatherings. If, as we have seen our priestly service includes proclaiming the gospel, then are our gatherings the place for evangelism or should it

---

33. J. Piper, 'Preaching as Worship: Meditations on Expository Exultation', *Trinity Journal* (16NS, 1995), 32.

happen elsewhere? Given that our gatherings are specifically to build us up as the body of Christ, and evangelism is the beginning of that task, there is no reason why a seeker sensitive service designed for the outsider cannot take its place alongside other kinds of gatherings.

Chapter Seven

Youth and the experience of the Holy Spirit
John Gray

Darren writes:

> The Holy Spirit descended upon my body in July … The feeling that enveloped my body is hard to describe. Warmth and comfort must suffice.

He goes on to tell us his daughter was born profoundly deaf. But, a couple of weeks after some people had prayed for his daughter she was healed. She now has hearing up to 90 decibels. Darren continues:

> The first time I heard her say 'Dad' or answer to 'Rachel', was one of great enjoyment; of relief; of hope. Looking back, it was enough proof to show God is a miracle worker.

Lynn writes:

> I have found … my missing link providing me with the metaphysical and spiritual way to wellbeing … I feel so full of love for myself and others.

M. King writes:

> I suffered from urinary incontinence for several years. Numerous tests and treatments failed to find a cause or cure. Medical experts told me I would have this problem for the rest of my life. I also suffered from chronic fatigue syndrome and multiple food and chemical sensitivities … I [am now] experiencing the great satisfaction of helping to heal others through the healing ability I acquired …

Norma Luz Diaz writes:

> After my serious car accident, one day I became very angry and said, 'Enough already, I'm not going to take any pain killers today'. That day, with much pain in my body I went to bed … After a few minutes I felt an enormous energy penetrating into my feet and into the top of my head, and then my entire body. The next day I was able to walk, and what a blessing it was, not to have any pain in my body.

Here are four testimonies that speak of powerful movements in a person's life. They speak of warmth, comfort, healing and wellbeing. A casual glance in bookshops and conference brochures will uncover many such testimonies. While they speak of powerful experiences, they do not testify to the same source of power. Darren is Darren Beadman and his testimony appeared in the *Sydney Morning Herald*.[1] In his half-page testimony Beadman tells of the 'long journey to salvation that [saw] him [swap] the saddle for the Holy Spirit'. Lynn is a disciple of Reiki, 'an ancient form of natural hands-on healing during which Universal Life Force Energy is transferred to self or others ... This is a technique so simple, a child can learn it.'[2] M. King speaks of Ki, or energy treatment.[3] Norma Luz Diaz is speaking about TaeUlJu, which is healing sound from the source of the Universe. These healing sounds are in harmony with the way of the coming New Age – the New Heaven and New Earth.[4] Each witness indicates they have been so impacted by a healing experience that they have now become evangelists for truth.

While Beadman may not be classified as a 'youth', and it is not clear how old are the others quoted, one thing is clear: they speak the language of our age. A language of postmodernism which says 'If I am passionate about something then I have truth'.[5] It is the slogan of the 1960s amplified: 'If it feels good do it'. Similar language was used by 16 year old Michael Davy in the 1997 September issue of *Rolling Stone*: 'We've come to get re-psyched, mate.' That is, Michael's purpose in attending Youth Alive was to have an experience that would tell him he was on the right path. While *Rolling Stone* reporter, Matthew Hall, says there were a few things which set Youth Alive apart from rock concerts in general, he still wrote:

> We could, however, have been at any rock concert held in Australia over the last 12 months ... guys milling around in packs ... shy teenage girls ... giggling when one of the boys breaks from his pack to strike up a conversation.

---

1. D. Beadman, 'Saving Darren Beadman' in *The Sydney Morning Herald* (26 December, 1997) 43.
2. B. Bultitude, Reiki: *The Usui System of Natural Healing* (Trinity Reiki Centre, Caringbah, NSW).
3. *Health Lecture and Ki (Energy) Treatment* (International Chun Do Sun Bup Inc, Chatswood, NSW).
4. *TaeUlJu Healing Meditation Workshop for Mind, Body and Spirit* (Sydney DoJang, Sydney, NSW), 12.
5. Compare B. Fryling, 'Being Faithful in this Generation: The Gospel and Student Culture at the End of the 20th Century. A Discussion Paper for the IFES World Assembly' (Saturday, 1 July, 1995), 4.32.

A similar assessment could be made of Darren Beadman's testimony. Remove the seven references to Jesus or the Holy Spirit and you are left with a testimony which could have been given by any New Ager who also speaks of warmth, comfort, healing. Interestingly, it was one of the New Agers quoted above who used biblical imagery: 'New Heaven and New Earth'.

All of this raises the question: How can you know if anyone is experiencing the Holy Spirit? Can you tell by the feeling you have? How do you know the Holy Spirit of the LORD of all heaven and earth is at work? Does the Holy Spirit manifest himself across the religious or technique spectrum?

These are important questions for the current youth generation who are growing up in a postmodern world. These are the questions a new breed of Pentecostal youth pastors are asking. Phil Dooley, the Youth Pastor from one of Australia's largest Pentecostal churches, told me of a camp he led for his youth at the beginning of 1998. On one night, a couple of hundred kids danced and moshed for 3 hours to just 3 songs. He and his team had searched the Scriptures beforehand for wisdom on dancing. Their conclusion: There is nothing wrong with dancing before God. After all, King David had done so. They then encouraged their kids to 'get into it' and enjoy the time – which they no doubt did. Phil Dooley said it was an awesome time.

I then asked him, 'How do you know that what took place was of the Holy Spirit and not just humanity enjoying dancing to music they liked?' He indicated that that was a question he was trying to fathom too. In the end he intimated that, because he had encouraged the kids to dance before the Lord – that is, in a God honouring way – then it was of the Holy Spirit. But in the end he said, 'Changed lives are the evidence of the movement of the Holy Spirit.' He also told me that he and his peers are thinking differently to their immediate forebears. The current youth pastor places less emphasis on the 'movement of the Holy Spirit in a public meeting' and more on changed lives. Once again, this raises crucial questions:

> How do you know you have experienced the Holy Spirit?
>
> How do you know the Holy Spirit of the LORD of all heaven and earth is at work?

'Gen T'

These questions are all the more crucial at the end of the 20th Century because we live in an increasingly postmodern world which is 'post-rational' and more affective and experiential. This is even more so for Gen T.

The name

Gen T is one of the labels used of the current 0–19 year olds. (Due to the novelty of Gen T what follows is a sketch only. Given there is often an overlap or 'grey line' between generations, we will need to draw on some of what we know of Gen X as well). The 'T' in Gen T stands for technology because of their familiarity with, and use of, technology. This is the generation that does not need to read manuals to program VCRs, according to US futurist Tom Blischock.[6] Other labels include 'Cyberkids', because they are spending more time on the WWW than watching TV; and ACES: Alienated, Cynical, Experimental, Savvy.[7]

The world culture

Whatever label we use, this age group are, more than any other generation, part of a world culture. In 1991, Dr D. F. Wells, Professor of Historical and Systematic Theology at Gordon-Conwell Theological Seminary, spoke of emerging 'world cliche culture':

> The same music the world over, or at least wherever modernisation has gone it is predominantly rock music. It is the same movies, and they are predominantly American. It is the same tribal dress and it is blue jeans and T-shirts. Doesn't matter where you can go in the world you can buy blue jeans and a T-shirt. It is the same menus the world over. Anywhere you want to go you can get pizza and American fried chicken ...

> It is a world cliche culture that actually belongs to no particular place. It is a whole set of values and of appetites that goes with that culture, that strikingly is about the same whether you encounter it in Los Angeles, or New York, or London, or Paris or Tel Aviv or Tokyo.[8]

That this culture has further emerged for Gen T is clear. *Teenmoods*, the Mojopartners' global research report, which identified Gen T as 'ACES', supports this conclusion. After interviewing 10,000 teenagers

---

6. Phone conversation between J. Gray and T. Blischock, 21 March, 1998.
7. *Sydney Morning Herald* (8 August, 1996), 28.
8. D.F. Wells, Western Region Clergy Conference, Sydney. Session No 1. 28 May, 1991.

from countries as diverse as Australia, China, Japan, US, Canada, France, India, Ecuador, Costa Rica, France and Germany the report claimed:

> Kids from all over the world can sit down and talk about common issues, like the latest Madonna video, and understand one another – that's never happened before.[9]

Teenmoods concluded the identifiers for ACES: Alienated, Cynical, Experimental, Savvy; were 'global reference points' adequately identifying Gen T.

This phenomenon is further enhanced by increasing technology, which is growing more powerful and accessible. Take global communication for example. According to Blischock, Gen T will have a common language (English on the WWW) and will be able to speak to each other for extended periods of time via the WWW at a fraction of the cost of even a local telephone call.[10]

Increased data access

Use of the WWW also translates into increased access to more information. When combined with super tools and search engines this will mean Gen T will have more information at their fingertips than any other generation. According to Blischock, they will then seek more 'objective data' to make decisions.

More entertainment

Gen T is proving Neil Postman's words true: 'we have moved from an age of exposition to an age of entertainment'.[11] Entertainment is very much an accepted facet of life. According to *Teenmoods*, for example, a key finding is that Gen T likes ads which are realistic, funny [and yet] entertaining and interesting to watch.[12] Overwhelmingly, they want techno fun but also instant gratification.[13] Sega World in Sydney's Darling Harbour has changed its line-up of attractions to meet the demands of these Cyberkids who are into entertainment.[14]

---

9. *NZ Herald* (14 August, 1996).
10. Gray and Blischock.
11. Fryling, 4.29.
12. *Sydney Morning Herald* (8 August, 1996), 28.
13. *The Australian* (20 August, 1997), 34.
14. *The Australian* (20 August, 1997), 34.

More experimentation

Their world is not limited to Cyberspace. More younger Gen Xers and the older Gen Ts increasingly participate in extreme sports like helicopter bungee jumping.[15]

Affective learners

In addition, postmodernity highlights the experiential. Learning tends to be more affective than rational.

Again, speaking of Gen X, Roxburgh argues that advertisers, for example, know that what they need to communicate is an *'experience'* (his emphasis). He continues, 'people are making decisions – coming to know how they ought to act or decide – through the intuitive, the affective, the experiential ... People are looking beyond the rational for alternative ways of knowing truth.' He goes on to point out that the Gen Xers who are walking this path are 'almost totally ... well educated, middle-class men and women who already have a stake in the dominant culture and have used its values to achieve status. They are rejecting that value system in the hope finding something different'.[16]

Desire for community

Even though there is an increasing sense of world culture, Gen T is an alienated generation. Their alienation has been accentuated by the increasing disintegration of the nuclear family. According to Hugh Mackay, Gen Xers [and Gen T?] will accentuate the fragmentation by their use of child-care facilities in which a child can spend up to 12,500 hours before starting school. This is only 500 hours less than a child will spend in 13 years of schooling.[17] Consequently, there is an increased desire for community.[18] This can be seen in the popularity of TV shows 'Friends' and 'Seinfeld' in which groups of friends seek to make it together. Fryling notes that while students continually feel alone they avoid it by being part of very important friendship circles.[19]

---

15. *Herald Sun* (8 August, 1996), 11.
16. A.J. Roxburgh, *Reaching a New Generation. Strategies for Tomorrow's Church* (Illinois: IVP, 1993), 42–44.
17. H. Mackay, *Generations: Baby Boomers, Their Parents and Their Children* (Sydney: Macmillan, 1997), 161.
18. *B & T News* (2 August, 1996).
19. Fryling, 4.33.

For a growing number of Gen T this friendship circle is found on the WWW where, Australian Psychologist Brent Waters suggests, 'teenagers often have their most meaningful conversations with friends.'[20] Hugh Mackay echoes these observations as he compares and contrasts the 'Lucky' Generation with both the Boomers and 'Options' [Gen X] Generations.[21]

Spiritual sensitivity

Writing of Gen X, Roxburgh argues this 'search for community is broader and more inclusive than a longing for human belonging, important as this is; it is reaching out past human beings to embrace nature. It is fundamentally a search for connectedness with all life. To miss this point is to miss the essential character of the value transformation occurring in our society.'[22] This, he says, reflects an increasing desire for Gen X to be connected 'spiritually'. They want to be connected to the 'whole' not just 'part' of life.

That could be no more well illustrated than in *The Celestine Prophecy*, a Top Ten book for well over 18 months in 1995–1997. While a work of fiction, it is clearly used as a vehicle to propagate a thoroughly postmodern New Age philosophy. It predicts that as we approach the end of the 20th century, people will become more and more dissatisfied with the modern way of life and will seek change. It speaks of how 1000 years ago the human race had a God-consciousness but, beginning 400 years ago, began to lose it. Our God-consciousness was superseded by science and technology which, in the end, robbed us of even our awareness of God. *The Celestine Prophecy* posits

> Working to establish a more comfortable type of survival has grown to feel complete in and of itself as a reason to live, and we've gradually, methodically, forgotten our original question ... we've forgotten that we still don't know what we're surviving for.[23]

In other words, there is a quest for spirituality again. We can see that in the increasing patronage of the Australian Body, Mind and Soul festivals. Fryling's observation reveals this is not restricted to Australia:

> In the Ivory Coast nine out of ten students have been in touch with the occult.

---

20. *Sydney Morning Herald* (24 January, 1998).
21. Mackay, 49.
22. Roxburgh, 55.
23. J. Redfield, *The Celestine Prophecy: An Adventure* (Sydney: Bantam Books, 1993), 26.

> In France, there are more registered witches than priests. Islam and the cults are gaining many adherents worldwide due to their discipline and aggressive recruiting while ancestral religions still strongly influence students from rural areas in Africa and Asia.[24]

Furthermore, Fryling argues the postmodern academic world no longer pretends to be atheistic but instead gropes to find spiritual significance.[25]

Given that Gen T has been born into this world and has now watched TV shows like 'Captain Planet' for 5 years or so, it is quite possible that what is true of Gen X will flow on to Gen T. As mentioned above, this exploration of spirituality is leading Gen X (and T?) to want to be connected with the whole of life. They want to be in touch with each other and the Gaia, the spirit of planet Earth.

(We could look at this in at least two ways. On the negative side, this desire is an age old one which found expression the cults of Abram's day (Joshua 24:2). On the positive side, this desire could be seen as a generation seeking to find REST. The REST of Genesis 2:3 which, biblically speaking, is to know and experience complete peace and harmony with our Creator, each other, his creation and within ourselves. We cannot explore this further here, but it would make an interesting paper.)

Leadership vacuum

It's worth adding at this point that currently there is a leadership vacuum. Mackay argues that in a world where insecurity is commonplace and the uncertainties of the current Gen X prevail, 'we are almost instinctively attracted to the confident voice; the strong leader; the person who seems to know what ought to be done. Moral vacuums', he says, 'yearn to be filled.'[26] This, he says, accounts for part of the growth of fundamental Pentecostalism. What he observes is part of a larger vacuum. Leighton Ford in his book *Transforming Leadership*[27] argues there is a general lack of leadership in the worldwide Church. But it's not restricted to the Church. Warren Bennis, highly respected business author and Distinguished Professor

---

24. Fryling, 4.33.
25. Fryling, 4.31.
26. Mackay, 190.
27. L. Ford, *Transforming Leadership*, (London: IVP, 1991).

of Business Administration at the University of Southern California, argues in his book *Why Leaders Can't Lead. The Unconscious Conspiracy Continues*[28] that there is a worldwide dearth of leadership.

If this is true, there is a great opportunity for Christian leaders, and in particular church leaders, to rise up and lead. And we should. We know the Word of God. We know where God is leading us. We know where we are going. We need to lead.[29] At least three generations are longing for clear leadership. Boomers, Gen X and now Gen T will listen and follow anyone who has a clear voice and a certain direction.

Implications

The combination of Gen T's increasingly obvious world culture, their love of entertainment, desire for community and longing for a 'wholesome' spiritual connectedness, and their affective learning style means Gen T is open to events which offer these things. Because there is a leadership vacuum then anyone who offers anything vaguely like this will be popular.

It is little wonder that large meetings where technology is utilised, in an environment of spirituality which has an entertainment ambience, are popular with youth.

Events like Youth Alive are a consciously-designed, tailor-made youth event.[30] The organisers of Youth Alive are very good at missiology at this point: they know the world of the people they are seeking to reach.

In this regard, mainliners need to become missiologically savvy. This has been the cry of a number of key players, for example, in Sydney

---

28. W. Bennis, *Why Leaders Can't Lead: The Unconscious Conspiracy Continues* (San Francisco: Jossey-Bass Publishers, 1989).
29. D.F. Wells has some incisive comments on leadership. He says 'Genuine leadership is a matter of teaching and explaining what has not been so well grasped, where the demands of God's truth and the habits of the culture pull in opposite directions. Genuine leadership is a matter of finding ways of reaching greater Christian faithfulness and offering greater Christian service. And the one flows from the other.' Later on he remarks, 'The fundamental requirement of the Christian leader is not a knowledge of where the stream of popular opinion is flowing but a knowledge of where the stream of God's truth lies. There can be no leadership without vision of both what the church has become and what, under God, it should be. Only a genuine leader has such a vision.' See D.F. Wells, *No Place For Truth or Whatever Happened to Evangelical Theology?* (Michigan: Eerdmans, 1993), 215–216.
30. See C. Caine, *Youth Alive NSW Regional Package: Philosophy, Policy and Procedures* (Castle Hill: Youth Alive, 1997).

Anglicanism over the last 40 years. In 1956 Diocesan Missioner, Bernard Gook, wrote to the then Archbishop saying 'Church is boring' [for youth]. That drum has been repeatedly beaten since then,[31] but unfortunately we have seen little increase in missiological savvy.

New Age gurus and circuit speakers like Anthony Robbins are also missiologically savvy.[32] Robbins and other New Age gurus can pull a larger crowd than Youth Alive doing all the same pragmatic things.

If larger, entertaining events is what counts then we could ask if Anthony Robbins is pouring out the Holy Spirit like Benny Hinn does (or like Elton John and Billy Joel did in their double act in Australia recently?). In each case audiences leave feeling warm and goose-bumped.[33] In all likelihood, though, it may simply be the 'magic of a large number gathered together to experience the same event'.

There is nothing wrong with this experience. The Old Testament indicates that at special times there were for example 120 trumpeters who played in God's Temple (2 Chronicles 5:12). King David provided 4,000 instruments for use in the Temple (1 Chronicles 23:5). In Revelation 5:11–14 we read of 'myriads of myriads and thousands of thousands' of angels singing to God along with the Elders and every living creature. There is little doubt that listening to them would have produced – or will produce – similar experiences to our large events.

---

31. In 1965, the retiring Youth Director of the Anglican Youth Department, John Turner, wrote in *The Southern Cross*, Vol. 5, N° 3 (March 1965), 8:
    the old-fashioned fellowship meeting was ... not really achieving its objective of helping young Christians in the study of the Scriptures, pray[ing] together show[ing] concern for missionary activity or mak[ing] the Gospel known to their contemporaries.
    Does the average teenager who has no previous connection with the Church since he drifted out of Sunday School, somewhere about the age of eleven, or 'graduated' after he was confirmed at 14, find Friday night in a drab Parish Hall the most thrilling experience of the week?
    He concluded:
    I am sure that if we are honest we will realise that we have a need to find a new basis for evangelism.
    Dudley Foord, now elder statesman in the Anglican Sydney scene, said in an interview with J. Gray, at Thornleigh NSW on May 6, 1993:
    Mediocrity attracts mediocrity and once you talk about evangelism you can't dissociate [it] from the local church. If the local church is dull and boring it KILLS evangelism' (His emphasis).
32. See *Sydney Morning Herald* (19 August, 1996) Agenda, 11.
33. That is certainly the testimony of friends who went to the John-Joel Sydney concert. It is also the testimony of those who have been to New Age seminars. See *Sydney Morning Herald* (19 August, 1996) Agenda, 11.

Our primary question, though, still stands: How do you know you have experienced the Holy Spirit? How do you know the Holy Spirit of he LORD of all heaven and earth is at work?

Experiencing the Holy Spirit

For the purposes of this paper we will look at just one passage of Scripture; Ephesians 5:15-6:10. It is chosen because (a) in it Paul teaches what are undisputed identifiers of the experience of the Holy Spirit and (b) the church to which he writes emerged from a world not too dissimilar to our postmodern New Age world.[34] Fundamentally, this passage consists of a command followed by four subordinate clauses. The command is expressed in verse 18:

> Do not get drunk with wine, for that is debauchery; but be filled with the Spirit.

Two caveats

1. Before we proceed we need remind ourselves to read this passage carefully. This is not because the Bible is unclear, but because over the years people have read and taught this command so poorly that what the Bible means is difficult to hear above the cacophony of wrong teaching.

Some, for example, have taught that to be filled with the Spirit is like being filled with wine – that is drunk with the Spirit as in Acts 2:15. This link has led some to conclude

> Now when grace fills the soul, that soul thereby rejoices and smiles and dances, for it is possessed and inspired, so that to many of the unenlightened it may seem to be drunken, crazy and beside itself ... the body is also fiery and flushed ... and thus many of the foolish are deceived and suppose that the sober are drunk ... and it is true that these sober ones are drunk in a sense.[35]

This sort of teaching comes from poor Bible reading, and when married to the spirit of our age courts disaster. You will note this teaching is not new. It has been around since Philo who lived 20 BC –

---

34. See Acts 19. Also C.E. Arnold, *Ephesians, Power and Magic: The Concept of Power in Ephesians in the Light of its Historical Setting* (Grand Rapids, Michigan: Baker Book House, 1992), 5–42.
35. Cited in A.T. Lincoln, *Ephesians Word Biblical Commentary* (Texas: Word Books, 1990), 344.

AD 40. Even theologian Gordon Fee highlights the disaster when he says:

> This was a common interpretation of my Pentecostal heritage, where the context was scarcely considered and the individual, personal experience of the Spirit was [paramount].[36]

The problem with the idea of 'getting drunk on the Spirit' is that this is not what Paul taught. He doesn't say 'get drunk with the Spirit'. He says 'be filled with the Spirit'. And, as we will see, there is a world of difference.

2. We also need to be careful how we use biblical language. In our world there is a tendency to latch onto biblical phrases, such as 'that is a spirit-filled person/church', and then to think we are speaking biblically because we use Bible words. This is a mistake. Speaking biblically is to use Bible words the way the Bible uses the words.

With these caveats in mind, we can now turn attention to the passage.

Walking

The command to be filled with the Holy Spirit is part of a much larger section in Ephesians which begins with Ephesians 4:1 and ends with Ephesians 6:9. The section is united by the repetition of one word which is translated 'live'. Live is not a bad word but the original word is far richer. It is the word 'walk' *(peripateo)* and conveys the idea of a step by step journey through life. Ephesians 4:1 is the great turning point of the letter. Chapters 1–3 look at the great salvation God has won for us in Christ. Chapters 4–6 provide the application, or practical outworking, of that salvation.

Chapters 4-6 spell out what it means to walk the faith. 4:1–16 teaches us to walk in community as we use our God-given gifts to build the Church. 4:17–5:1 warns us not to walk as pagans/gentiles do.[37] Ephesians 5:1-14 tells us we are to walk a life of love.

---

36. G.D. Fee, *God's Empowering Presence: The Holy Spirit in the Letters of Paul* (Peabody, MA: Hendrickson Publishers, 1994), 721 footnote 195.
37. The contrast is between evil dark ways of pagan life and the life of God's people. Life is to be distinctive to pre-converted days. This is a highly significant comparison for the Ephesians, who were converted out of a magic background. In Acts 19:19 we are told those converted in Ephesus burned 50,000 drachmas (about $5 million dollars worth) of magic books. The Ephesians' background is not too dissimilar to current New Age environments.

With each use of the word 'walk' we are introduced to a contrast: the old way of walking and the new. The new is always presented in terms of godliness: love, truth, purity, morality, unity. This is the way God's people are to walk. This is the direction of the tide in Ephesians 4:1–6:9. It is in this context that we see the last use of 'walk' in Ephesians 5:15–18. Again, there is a contrast between the old way of walking and the new.

> Be careful then how you live *(peripateite)*, not as unwise people but as wise, making the most of the time, because the days are evil. So do not be foolish, but understand what the will of the Lord is. Do not get drunk with wine, for that is debauchery; but be filled with the Spirit.

Drunkenness is foolishness or pure folly. It is to be completely lacking in self control. In fact, drunkenness is a mark of living in the darkness (compare 1 Thessalonians 5:7). We are not to be like that. Instead, we are to be wise men and women who are filled with the Spirit (5:18). Being filled with the Spirit therefore has to do with living, or walking, in new life. Before we can specifically identify what characterises this aspect of our walk, we need to note three things which will help us.

The command

Firstly, this is a command. It is not an optional extra for God's people. This fact is reinforced in the Greek by use of the plural for you. The sense is of 'you as group of God's people' are to be filled with the Holy Spirit. In other words, being Spirit-filled is not just for the super-spirituals. It is to be the norm for all of God's people.

An ongoing process

Secondly, we need to note the tense of the command. In English we're familiar with past, present and future tenses: she ran, she runs, she will run. There is, however, another tense: the present continuous. An example might be 'she is running'. Ephesians 5:18(b) is a command in the present continuous. That is, we are to be in the process of being filled with the Holy Spirit. It is therefore a command we can never complete.

It is like the command to love our neighbour. If we are very good at it for a moment there is still another moment and another neighbour. It always lies ahead of you and is always applicable to you. If you are filled with the Spirit today that is good. But tomorrow is another day. We are to go on being filled with the Holy Spirit and therefore always obeying Ephesians 5:18.

A passive command

Thirdly, the command is in the passive voice. Bible translators get the sense using the English word 'be': not 'fill yourselves' but 'be filled'. Of course, this leads to an important question: how can we obey a command that we cannot do for ourselves? What do I need to do? Pray? Yield? What?

Paul does not tell us do any of that. If he wanted us to 'do' anything he would have made that very clear as he did on other occasions.

The emphasis in a passive command is not on what you have to do but on what God is doing to you. This is where the contrast to being drunk comes in again. The command is to be filled by the Spirit. That is, let the fullness you have be that which the Spirit produces not what alcohol produces. Let your manner of life be that which the Spirit produces.

What does that look like? By way of contrast, to see what it does **not** look like, look at a drunken man. He staggers, lurches, leers, sings at the top of his voice, his speech can be slurred, he reeks of alcohol. Some get violent. Some get all sooky.

So, how do you know?

How do you know you have experienced the Holy Spirit? How do you know the Holy Spirit of the LORD of all heaven and earth is at work? Paul leaves us in no doubt for he goes on from the command to write Ephesians 5:19–21. Most English translations have not fully captured what Paul wrote. Except for the NASB or NRSV, translations end the command at verse 18. Most make verses 19–21 a new paragraph. But in Paul's pen the command continues into verse 19–21. Paul states the command and then writes four subordinate clauses, each of which explain what is meant by the command. Verses 19–21 tell us what a Spirit-filled person looks like. Such a person is identified by four characteristics.

Speaking to one another in songs

They speak to one another in song. This does not mean they have a sing-song quality to their voice. It means that when they sing songs (in church/Christian gatherings?) they sing God's truth to one another. They teach one another truth as they sing songs together.

The emphasis is on horizontal relationships. If we do this well Paul tells us we will teach and admonish one another (Colossians 3:16). Incidentally, this means we need to make sure the content of songs is the truth of Scripture. At times this will no doubt feel great particularly if the band and music is 'hot'. At other times it may not feel so great (like when the band and the music is not so 'hot'). There may be times when it will not feel great when those present sense an admonition from God. But Spirit-filled people obey Ephesians 5:18 and sing to please their heavenly Father.

Making music with all our hearts to God

Horizontal singing is not the only dimension to our singing. According to verse 19(b) there is also a vertical dimension. That is, when we sing songs we are to sing them 'with all our heart' (NIV) to the LORD God: Jesus. As always, the Spirit will help us focus on Jesus Christ. Paul is no armchair teacher here. He knew what it was to suffer for being a Christian (compare Acts 16:22–25; 2 Corinthians 11:16–33). In Acts 16:25 Paul was not singing because he was in jail. He and Silas sang because they knew God. A Spirit-filled person does not focus on the circumstances which surround him/her. Instead they remember and recall how great God has been to them. They recall the rich blessings of Christ which Paul outlined in the one exuberant sentence of Ephesians 1:1–14 and they sing to God. It is worth noting at this point that in Acts 16:22–24 we are told that Paul and Silas had been attacked by an angry crowd, stripped and 'severely flogged' (with whips?) and placed in stocks in prison. No one would suggest they were feeling good and warm inside. Yet they were clearly filled with the Spirit as they sang praise to God. They had taken their focus off their circumstances and remembered God.

These first two characteristics of a Spirit-filled person mean that when we sing we need to be mindful of who we are singing to, and when. Sometimes a song is addressed to God, to us, to both God and us. Often Psalms, for example, have two dimensions. See for example Psalm 30 in which verse 1–3 focus on God, verse 4–5 call to the believer and verse 6–9 focus back on God. This can also be seen in some contemporary songs like 'Shout to the Lord' in which the verse focuses on God and the chorus on the people of God.

Through it all we sing truth which is of benefit to all who hear. Even songs which address God alone are teaching tools for they remind us of our great God. And that can be a great encouragement to people who are doubting or worried or wondering if God still loves them.

Just as you can tell if a man is drunk by what he sings, so you can tell a Spirit-filled person by what s/he sings.

Thanking God

The third characteristic of Spirit-filled men or women is their thankful attitude (Ephesians 5:19–20(a)). A thankful outlook stands in stark contrast to many an Australian Christian. You can get a glimpse of this contrast as you listen to prayers. Thanksgiving appears to be such a small part while the 'shopping list' is quite long. If this is true it reflects a self-centred approach to life which is evidence of the 'old life'. We are to be living a new life. Those who continually grumble about life, spouse and job are not obeying the command of Ephesians 5:18. Certainly, there may be issues to work through. But this is not to be an excuse for a lack of obedience to Ephesians 5:18. Sometimes people will feel great as they offer thanks because they are emotionally connected with the thanksgiving. At other times they may not feel like it, as Paul and Silas may not have felt like it in Acts 16. But giving thanks is a mark of one filled with the Spirit and expected of all Christians (compare 1 Thessalonians 5:18) Thanksgiving is a mark of one living the new Spirit-filled life.

Submitting to one another

The final characteristic of one filled with the Spirit is found in verse 21: submission to other brothers and sisters. We are to submit to Jesus and every other Christian who is submitting to Jesus. And this is the reverse of the world's thought patterns.

Submission is not only the fourth mark on the gauge but also the largest mark on the gauge. Paul spends Ephesians 5:22–6:9 unpacking what it means to submit to each other. He speaks of relationships between husbands and wives, parents and children, slaves and masters (in our day this could be applied to relationships in the workforce).

As we are looking at youth and the Holy Spirit, this section is of particular importance. A Spirit-filled youth/child obeys his/her parents which entails honouring father and mother (Ephesians 6:1–3). Here is one who knows they are being filled with the Holy Spirit. Life is radically changed for a boy-man or girl-woman who is struggling with what it means to make the transition from childhood to adulthood. As they make this transition they will do so in a Christlike manner which will honour parents.

Once again, at times this may not feel good and warm as the tensions and exasperation of becoming an adult physically, emotionally and psycho-socially are experienced. There is even the very real fear, for Gen X and Gen T Christians from a non-English speaking background, that they may be rejected and disowned by their families for following Christ. There is the deep emotional turmoil of working out how to honour parents who have a Buddhist faith, for example, and also helping such parents see they are actually being honoured. But people filled with the Spirit obey Ephesians 5:18 as they seek to live out Ephesians 6:1–3. Such obedience will no doubt encourage Christian parents as they see the Spirit at work in their children. Hopefully, it will cause non-Christian parents to ask why their offspring are living like Christ (and come to faith themselves).

What the apostle Paul teaches about the evidence of one's experience of the Holy Spirit radically differs from the testimony of New Agers and those who have warm and comforting feelings. (As intimated above there is a place for these feelings. They are just not evidence of the experience of Holy Spirit). What Paul teaches as clear experiences of the Holy Spirit is very different to the experiences of large youth events. Experiencing the Holy Spirit is evidenced by a changed life regardless of warm and comforting feelings.

From one perspective the Spirit-filled life is not spectacular. It's not like you walk down the street and say 'Look at that!' The Spirit-filled Christian does not necessarily look like the New Age gurus, or others dripping with the accoutrements of success. The Spirit-filled Christian may not always feel good and warm inside.

From another perspective, and, I would submit, a biblical perspective, the Spirit-filled life **is** spectacular. Who in this world resembles Ephesians 5:19–21? Only God's people. When the people of God are Spirit-filled they are very impressive indeed. Such people walk differently to the world, love differently to the world, serve differently to the world.

These people are connected with the Creator God of all heaven and earth not just some phantom of the earth called Gaia. They are connected with the community of people who live forever and who, when they serve one another, experience the removal of alienation and fear. This community is an eschatological community. It looks forward to Christ's return because it knows that no matter how good it may get here, this is not Home. Full heavenly status will not be enjoyed this side of Christ's return. So through the 'tension of the two ages', this community seeks to live under the Lordship of Christ, in the power of the Holy Spirit, looking to the Father. Such a community gets a taste of heaven for they see what it means to be a biblically functioning people of God.

Such a people are a very impressive people who can be developed regardless of the technology available. (The Ephesian church did not have anything like that which is available to us, and this is great news for those who don't have video projectors, lights or amplifiers.) It is a community of integrity and authenticity in which truth is taken seriously and lives are radically transformed by that truth. It a community that is very attractive to Gen T who are alienated, looking for community and a life worth living. Gen T will live Ephesians 6:1–3. If they marry they will enter marriage with the power and knowledge to reverse the divorce rate because, filled with the Holy Spirit, they will live Ephesians 5:22–33. When they become parents they will be parents filled with the Spirit who will not exasperate their children. Such a generation will not search for community in gangs or chat rooms. Instead they will seek for it in the community of God's people.

Only in such a community as this will youth experience the Holy Spirit.

CHAPTER EIGHT

A relational theology of youth ministry
Peter Hotchkin

What are the key elements of the best youth ministry or youth group you have been involved with? If asked that question, most people answer in terms of the relationships and interactions characterising the group or groups within their experience. Issues of programs, activities, locations and sometimes even leaders take a back seat to the relationship-dynamics of the group. At the National Anglican Youth Gathering in Brisbane (January 1996) the word *community* was continually raised. And what is community, except a collective description of relationship? Bishop George Browning suggested that the entire group was a community, but within that, there were residential communities; discussion group communities; duty group communities; communities of friends; and that God was a community: The Trinity. Central to the faith of the Church is the doctrine of the Trinity: 'We worship one God in Trinity, neither confounding the Persons: nor dividing the Substance'.[1]

Generally what we say about our youth ministries would include the clichés we have learned: *Relationships are vital; Treat each young person with respect; Who you are as a person is more important than what you do.* But I suspect that this is token assent and not truly our *owned* Theology of Youth Ministry. We do not always mean it! If you only gain one point from this paper may it be this: Do not give token assent to anything you say about Youth Ministry – but actually mean it!

The theological significance of our interpersonal relationships should not be overlooked. It is by the example of our Lord Jesus Christ that we learn to embrace relationships with others as among the most important elements of our applied faith. Indeed, Jesus taught that our choice to follow demanded our commitment to pure, impeccable interpersonal relationships with others.

---

1. The Creed of Athanasius, *A Prayer Book for Australia* (Alexandria: Broughton Books, E.J. Dwyer, 1995), 487.

When asked to define the greatest commandment, Jesus answers, 'You shall love the Lord your God with all your heart, and with all your soul and with all your mind.' This is the greatest and first commandment. And a second is like it: 'You shall love your neighbour as yourself.'[2] Ponder how Jesus answers with *two*. Why would that be? Could it be the second issue was so important that trying to live by the first commandment alone would not be enough? And why did Jesus say the second was *like it*? How is loving our neighbour *like* loving God?

Jesus declares that relationships are more important than our religious practices and activities: 'So when you are offering your gift at the altar, if you remember that your brother or sister has something against you, leave your gift there before the altar and go; first be reconciled to your brother or sister, and then come and offer your gift.'[3] In other words, stop doing your religious thing and get your relationship right!

An Anglican approach to youth ministry

What is unique about Anglican youth ministry? Is an Anglican youth ministry different to another youth ministry? I think it ought to be: 'The beliefs of Anglicanism (*or perhaps one could say our theology*) are common to the Christian faith – the Bible, the creeds – but it is in the focus or living out of those beliefs that Anglicanism differs'.[4] Anglicanism is focused on the Incarnation of God, through Jesus Christ. 'This doctrine declares that God revealed himself in a particular time and place – a time and place which were unique and distinct yet nonetheless part of the continuous flow of the human condition, in which God has never ceased to be an intimate participant.'[5] Consistent with the theme of this conference, it is vital that we grasp the theology of the incarnation embraced within the Trinity: that Jesus is indeed God and that Jesus is indeed the human incarnation of God, conceived by the Holy Spirit as we are taught in the Apostles' Creed.[6] At the same time, the Trinity is one of the great mysteries of the Christian faith – which in our present lives we can only hope to see and understand as in a mirror, dimly.[7]

---

2. Matthew 22:37–39.
3. Matthew 5:23–24.
4. Bishop Bruce Wilson (Bathurst) 1997 *Synod President's Address*
5. Bruce Kaye, *A Church Without Walls*, (Australia: HarperCollins Religious, 1995), 6.
6. 'The Apostles' Creed', *APBA*, 12.
7. 1 Corinthians 13:12.

I am convinced that it is because of God's great love for us that we were even considered for salvation. God loves us with such an all-accepting and overwhelming love that we are saved by this love – first! Because God loves us – God saves us. This belief is at direct odds with the concept that God saves us to love us. That is to say that 'when God looks at me, God sees not me, but sees Jesus.' God is not so easily fooled! God does not save us first, and love us second. We are not *saved* by double imputation but by the love of our Creator God, choosing us – as St Paul said 'while we were still sinners'.[8] The Old Testament prophet Hosea was told to marry a prostitute as an example of how the Israelites were living. Yet God still chose to love them – and us – while in a sinful, broken state – not in a redeemed and sanctified state. Why is this important as a theological foundation? We ought also to love our clients as God loves us.

Jesus within us

Most Christians would not argue that we carry within us the presence of God and therefore Jesus and the Holy Spirit. The Trinity is at work and is indeed present within our lives. There may be some disagreement about how it gets there, and some of us may doubt or question the validity of this in other's lives. We might certainly disagree about the definitions, but the statement that Jesus is present in the lives of believers is undisputed. We could conclude, wherever a person of Christian faith ministers to young people it is Jesus who works through his/her life to minister, work and bring about change in the lives of those young people. In a way, no matter what the ministry model, Christians minister through a Trinitarian approach (God, in Jesus through the Holy Spirit within our lives).

Jesus in others

A greater challenge is to seek to see Jesus in the lives of others. In particular, to see Jesus in the lives of broken, fallen, unChristian young people. It is an unsettling and confronting concept. Yet we cannot ignore the importance of looking past their faces to recognise the significance of each person.

> It means that where anyone, child, man, woman, criminal, physically or mentally handicapped person, atheist, agnostic, Hindu, divorcee, lesbian;

---

8. Romans 5:8.

where anyone, however, fragile, however lonely, however bitter, however dehumanised, comes in touch with us as Christian community we are to meet them as Christ (*Them as Christ – not us as Christ*): not with ponderous, earnest, do-gooding welcomes, intent on their reformation or conversion; not with pity or condescension. Rather to meet them as a gift, as part of the mystery of creation, in the expectancy of new discovery, new disclosure of the meaning of our common humanness.[9]

C.S. Lewis asserted this same principle:

> It is a serious thing to live in a world of possible gods and goddesses, to remember that the dullest and most uninteresting person you can talk to may one day be a creature which, if you saw it now, you would be strongly tempted to worship, or else a horror and a corruption such as you now meet, if at all, only in a nightmare. All day long we are, in some degree, helping each other to one or the other of these destinations. It is in the light of these overwhelming possibilities, it is with the awe and the circumspection proper to them, that we should conduct all our dealings with one another, all friendships, all loves, all play, all politics. There are no ordinary people. You have never talked to a mere mortal. But it is immortals who we joke with, work with, marry, snub and exploit – immortal horrors or everlasting splendours – no flippancy, no superiority, no presumption. And our charity must be a real costly love, with deep feeling for the sins in spite of which we love the sinner – no mere tolerance, or indulgence which parodies love as flippancy parodies merriment. Next to the Blessed Sacrament itself, your neighbour is the holiest object ever presented to your senses.[10]

Mother Teresa said, 'Jesus comes to us as the sick and the homeless, he comes to us in the distressing disguise of the poor.'[11]

Bishop Richard Holloway (Primus of Scotland), similarly challenged people to be radically accepting of others, and leave the work of getting peoples lives tidied up to God.[12]

Jesus said, 'Truly I tell you, just as you did it to one of the least of these who are members of my family, you did it to me.'[13] So I challenge you: how are you treating Jesus as you encounter him every day? He is incarnate in the lives of others who may well be fallen, lost or unsaved.

---

9. Elizabeth Templeton, National Anglican Conference handbook (1997), 46.
10. C.S. Lewis, *The Weight of Glory* (New York: Collier Books Macmillan, 1980), 18–19.
11. Mother Teresa, 'The Poor in Our Midst', *New Covenant Magazine* (January 1977), 15–77.
12. Church for Tomorrow seminar (Melbourne, 1997).
13. Matthew 25:40. Please read verses 31–46.

There is no difference in the quality of person between Christians and non-Christians. We are not better or more complete people because of our faith. If you think you are, then you have not grasped the doctrine of atonement at all. No matter which way you look at atonement – it is about how we as sinners are saved by a sinless God. It is about how God makes atonement for our sins, not how we can lift ourselves up by our own bootstraps to become acceptable to God by believing a set of rules or doctrine, however orthodox!

The best example of a human being was Jesus Christ. God incarnate! Often we think about humanity in terms of how Christian we may be. Perhaps, when we look at the human condition, it may help us to see that our salvation is not the epitome of the human condition. That honour is to Christ alone. We are, at our very best, only ever forgiven sinners! All of us! So we ought not to think more highly of ourselves.

Working with real young people, in a real world, we do not have to worry about the possibility of idolising our clients because we approach them as if they are Christ. It is not long before their truly fallen state is revealed. It takes great effort to remind ourselves of Christ's words about the least of these – just as it takes great effort to remind ourselves that we are not superior because of our faith. The danger, I think, is that we will idolise ourselves, not our clients.

Jesus encounters

Jesus was a truly astounding person. People around him believed even just to touch his clothes would bring healing within their lives. I want you to think about why it is that someone would think that about another person. I believe it is because they perceived that Jesus cared about people. That Jesus was truly concerned about others, no matter what their spiritual state during or after the encounter. Jesus is a great exemplar of this sort of Relational Ministry.

It is unfortunate that Jesus was not a good evangelist. In the parable of the Good Samaritan, Jesus simply told the lawyer to go and be a good neighbour. Jesus neglected to espouse the four spiritual laws or to inform the lawyer that he was, in fact, God incarnate. The vital fact that salvation rests in Jesus alone was totally ignored.[14] Instead, the

---

14. Rebecca Manley Pippert, *Out of the salt shaker* (Leicester: Inter-Varsity Press, 1979).

issue of relationships was raised as central to the lawyer's salvation.[15]

Jesus applied the rules evenly to both himself and humanity. So if Jesus told us to forgive 'seven times seventy' when someone sins against us then that rule applies also to God. That forgiveness is given as often as we require it. That is pretty refreshing to me. I met someone once who said they struggled when they first became a Christian but in recent years had gained victory over sin and had not sinned for a few years now. I acknowledged their faithfulness but felt they had missed the point a bit. We seem to have an unhealthy obsession with sin. Sin becomes more of a focus than the love and forgiveness of God. The importance of our relationships is given a low priority. Would it not be more healthy to allow the love of God to enfold us? God's overwhelming and radically forgiving love could then become the focus of our lives, allowing us freedom to express that love to others through our relationships.

That does not mean that we neglect spiritual discipline and obedience. Jesus' life and teachings challenge us to obedience. We are to be faithful to God and the calling on our lives. But faithfulness does not simply mean adhering to a set of teachings and behaviours. Jesus calls us to a radical religion of the heart: a changed heart, a focus without (rather than within) and obedience to radical teachings of love, inclusion and forgiveness.

Applied to ministry models

However, I have promised to apply this theology to four ministry models I have observed in a little over ten years in full-time youth ministry.

Camping Ministry

During my teen years I attended Baptist Youth Camps in Western Australia. These camps generally had the major purpose worked out. The target group was churched young people yet there was an evangelistic approach, resulting in lots of recommitments to Christ. There was a fun program, great facilities and adequate leaders. Looking back, I can highlight these camps as somewhat meaningful times in my faith development. I could criticise some of the strategies used by

---

15. See Luke 10:25–37.

speakers, leaders and directors, strategies such as building an environment of judgment; manipulating young people to feel guilt in unwarranted situations; criticism of questioning; coercing people to attend optional prayer meetings. I could commend strategies such as discussion groups, nightly devotions, some of the room group leaders' willingness to listen and counsel young people. The program was well developed and the camps were fun.

But with all the talks I have heard over many years, and all the people who would have been leaders for me at that time – all that remains is the key relationships where leaders actually made an effort to accept me, involve me and follow up after the camp. The most significant individual who did this was not one of the room group leaders but a kitchen hand – with whom I still have contact. During the camp, we became friends even though some of my behaviour and lifestyle at that time would have been considered unacceptable. He had gone a little further along the journey and was prepared to devote time to having a real relationship with me – not because he had to but because he considered me to be a friend. It is that relationship which is foremost in my mind when I reflect on the ministry I received through those camps.

I went on to be a leader at those camps. I also acted as a leader on Youth For Christ (YFC) camps run by other staff members. The underlying purpose of these camps remained the same and I was not particularly skilled at giving 'good Christian answers'. I realised at an early age the 'pat answers' Christians often give do not work. I was also certain that I had not arrived at a destination in my faith journey, although I could not articulate this at that stage. Consequently, I never fitted the description of an ideal leader. I always had too much fun, led a room group to play some trick or practical joke or got asked by the director to 'turn it down a bit'. I liked to hang around talking and did not seem committed to getting to the program activities on time.

This was instinctive practice of the theology of relationships. At that stage, I had not identified this ministry strategy but knew enough that it was in being *real* I could both relax and influence others too.

When it came to the end of a camp, everyone would be signing autograph books or camp journals. It was in this area that my failure as a leader was most obvious. At the end of camps, leaders often signed their name and gave the campers some gem of a Bible verse. I could never remember a reference the way good leaders did. They just seemed to know what to write to whom and were always able to remember the best verses. Maybe they were inspired by God or led by the Spirit... but not me. I failed! I don't think I have ever looked up one of those references that other people gave me, but it always annoyed me that I could not think of even one reference to write. I just wrote my phone number ...

When I began running camps for YFC a few years later, I trained my leaders just to write their phone number! I knew the potential of camping ministry to influence, challenge and change the lives of young people. But I believed the best way to do it was through a theology of relationships. I developed a camping ministry through the Youth Guidance department of YFC.

My camps were quite different in their approach. The campers were usually 'unchurched' and under my leadership, the primary focus was on building real, personal and significant relationships with the campers in each room group. Leaders were encouraged, indeed asked to follow up and spend time with the campers. My team was second to none! Some former team members have gone on to work in Christian ministries, government youth work and social welfare agencies. Others are now running the camping program since I have moved on.

The success of the Youth Guidance camping program is linked to the focus on building relationships. This model did bring young people to make Christian commitments or have a conversion experience. But more important to me was the integrity of the ministry in presenting an authentic Christian life. More important was the acceptance of campers who had been thrown out by other church organisations. For we tried to accept everyone, as they were! Although at times I had to send young people home from a camp because of disruptive behaviour, there was still an underlying value of acceptance. One camper named Michael was sent home from a camp, but we kept contact and let him come back on the next one. Through maintaining a relationship Michael went on to become one of the junior leaders and a trusted part of the leadership team.

If we cast aside our own piety and purity (as God did in Christ); if we become truly human (as God did in Christ); then we are becoming Christlike ... 'like the Christ of the synoptic Gospels – who deliberately took the side of the marginalised and oppressed, who opposed the religious establishment of the day, who proclaimed the all-inclusive and transforming good news of God's reign, who emphasised justice and mercy in human community and who found less faith in all Israel than he did in the Gentiles he encountered'.[16]

Just as Jesus left a bunch of meandering no-hopers in charge of extending the reign of God, my own ministry really took off when I learned that valuable lesson; take risks on relationships and people who are not squeaky clean. On the way to a leadership camp once, one volunteer asked if she was supposed to be a Christian to be a leader. Now for YFC that was official policy! I had invited a leader on camp who was not a Christian by any measure and never claimed to be! If this news travelled back to the powers that be, there would be quite a negative reaction. Yet I believed that this person had something to offer and something to gain by coming along. Jenny Moloney now works for Uniting Church Family Services. She is making a huge contribution to the lives of many young people and participating in the life of the wider church. All because I made a mistake? No, because I employed the principle of a relational theology of ministry.

City wide club

From the camping ministry grew a regular youth group or club ministry. The Youth Guidance ministry was for a specific target group. We chose to work with teenagers from outcast and marginalised backgrounds: single parent families, referrals from police and government agencies. These were arguably the bottom twenty five per cent of society in socioeconomic terms. Our work was never to convict them (or make them feel convicted) of sin so we developed a non-judgmental environment at club, something many church youth groups lack. We did not judge actions, language, comments or behaviour, so young people felt included within the group. The focus was on the person and keeping a real relationship; being tolerant and accepting. However, the greatest impact I personally made (apart from running the program that facilitated volunteer leaders to minister to youth) was in dropping people home. I literally spent four hours each club night in the bus, driving teenagers to their homes and talking along the way. It was at these times the relationships were built. Teenagers do not understand the concept of quality time because quality time is a

---

16. Mike McCoy 1998 (Inter Mission).

management myth! What counts in the minds of young people is the sheer quantity of time it takes to build a real relationship.

Parish youth ministry

Having worked as a youth ministry consultant in the diocese of Brisbane and as an employed parish youth minister in Melbourne I have observed various parish situations. Those instances where youth ministry was successful were where the parish concentrated effort on building relationships with and among young people.

Many parishes, for various motives, want a Youth Ministry program but not relationships with young people. Some parishes, while actively hostile towards young people, claim they desire to minister to youth! Little can be done to help these parishes. You can give some training and ideas for reaching out to young people, but while the mentality endures that the program or activity is more important than relationships with the people, nothing of substance can develop.

Parish youth ministry seems to be plagued by issues such as lack of support or involvement in leadership, or the expectation that a super-leader will relieve adults of any obligation towards the youth. Sometimes adults within a congregation manipulate or criticise the youth. I have seen young people whose lives were so together that they would be better youth mentors than many of us (in terms of unpretentious Christian living) – yet these young people knelt at the rails in church weeping uncontrollably because they felt unacceptable to God. Youth who ran prayer meetings at school, on their own initiative, without even a suggestion from adults. Youth who prayed with their non-Christian friends and led them to Christian faith! Youth who read their Bibles and maintained exemplary personal devotional lives. They actually did all the things that we youth workers tell young people to do but often do not do ourselves. It was sad to see the leadership of the parish minimise the positive aspects in these young people's lives, instead breeding an environment of guilt, fear and non-acceptance. The strength of this group came from within. Support came from within. The strong bonds of friendship empowered the group to exist and grow in faith. It was the relationships within the group that made it dynamic.

Being a Christian person in secular youth work

I have always maintained close links with community youth workers. I believe it is vital for the church to hold relationships within the youth sector. It took me years of *being* to build relationships and respect from secular youth workers. Being in youth work long term, and continuing my own program while building bridges to these people, is part of the holistic approach to youth ministry. I believe it is also important to attend secular youth sector events, do short courses, learn from these people as well as make comments from our own experience at their forums.

Many secular youth workers are feeling exactly like we do if we care to admit it. They experience both frustration and success. They must deal with the stress of working with people. I find it sad that Christian youth workers often see secular youth workers as an enemy to be feared or as humanists who have taken God out of our programs and re-used the same package. We should be building relationships with these people and consider working together.

One area of difference between Christian youth workers and our secular counterparts is not just our belief but also our relationship with God. We believe in someone or something bigger than ourselves, bigger than our problems, bigger than the pain and hurt that we see in the lives of young people. That always enables me to cope as I work with young people in crisis. The burnout rate for secular youth workers is very high. Many of the contacts I built with workers in Brisbane were short-lived. It is sad to see people who have become acquaintances crumbling under the stress of the occupation.

Young people recognise the difference between a real relationship and a work relationship. While secular youth workers are building relationships with their clients, there is sometimes a missing element in that relationship. Through building a real relationship with young people I would often find them telling me about their social or government youth worker, and how the teenager would 'string them along a bit'. I believe it was the perceptiveness of youth to distinguish between a real relationship and a work relationship that afforded them the confidence to tell me about their social worker. If they were stringing me along they also knew that I wasn't taking myself too seriously, as they felt their social worker sometimes did.[17]

In an outer suburban area of Melbourne, I had the pleasure of visiting the local schools with the council youth workers one day, and with a Student Focus club another day. Each of these models has strengths and weaknesses. Yet it was challenging to see the specific objective of each of these models.

I found the secular youth workers were more focused on building relationships. Their objective was to practise the principle of creatively hanging around and being there to develop relationships (and be available to talk) with young people. Some of the workers were more effective than others, but there was certainly a spiritual element missing from their approach. In contrast, the Christian youth workers became caught up in the programs and many relationship opportunities were lost.

Naturally, this is not an exhaustive theological evaluation of each of these models. There will be flaws in the argument and exceptions to the rule. However, I hope that you grasp the issue of the theology of relationships! You will find, if your objective is to see large numbers of young people brought to salvation, then the most effective way to do it is through cultivating real, personal relationships with people. Or if you are concerned with the social needs of young people and helping them through turbulent times as an extension of your caring for the community, then following Jesus' example of putting relationships first will effectively achieve the task. Our ministry models (whatever they are) should focus on the dynamic relationships within our ministry. But we need to be certain of why! Not just because it works, but because we see the principles of relationships within our ministry. Because we see the principles of relationship and community within our faith and within our God. Jesus constantly preached about relationships. God is in relationship within the Trinity. We would do well to follow this example.

---

17. Similar to the movie *Good Will Hunting*, where Will, not wanting to go through therapy, systematically goes through a number of psychologists until he meets one who will not play the game, who invites him back, who does not take himself seriously – but does take Will seriously.

CHAPTER NINE

Dying for a reason to live -
Youth suicide, and the search for meaning and belonging

Brad Lovegrove

One of the most serious social issues facing young people, and those who care about them, is the current rate of youth suicide. How might a Trinitarian theology be applied to this issue? I will first outline several sociological insights on the issue, then examine them from a Trinitarian perspective. Although it is not the purpose of this paper to address the moral or ethical question of the act of suicide, I will begin with a brief summary of how suicide has been viewed through history.

Sociological insights

Suicide – sin, sickness or solution?

Suicide has been described as a weakness, a noble act, a sin, a crime, a disease, and a natural choice. The question is at least as old as the Greek philosophers, and it was discussed at length by Homer, Pythagoras, the Stoics, and the Epicureans. The topic was of surprisingly little concern, however, to the biblical writers, who did not seem to think of it as a moral or ethical issue. There are few incidents of suicide in the Bible (Judges 9:54, 16:28–30; 1 Samuel 31:1–4; 2 Samuel 17:23; 1 Kings 16:18; Matthew 27:3–5) and they are reported without moral judgment.

Self-sacrifice and martyrdom were fairly common occurrences in the early church, and there may have even been a belief that imitating Christ's example literally meant imitating his sacrificial death. It was because some were seeking martyrdom too easily that Augustine took the position that suicide is an affront to God, as only he has the right to take away the life he has given (Job 1:21). In the following centuries the church took an increasingly strong position against suicide. That attitude began to shift with Thomas More, John Donne, Hume and

Kant, who began to think of suicide as an aberration of mind, to be treated tolerantly, as a disease.

Most questions of ethics assume a rational state of mind. If it is possible to be suicidal rationally, then the ethical question becomes relevant. However, many hold that suicidal behaviour is always a sign of emotional and mental distress, and often a cry for help. If suicidal behaviour is defined as evidence *per se* of mental derangement, then the person is to be forgiven rather than condemned (studies show 70% of suicides were depressed and 15% were alcoholic; while the Victorian Suicide Prevention report says depression features in 60–90% of suicide attempts).[1]

No doubt there are also suicides motivated by sinful, selfish goals such as punishing others or attention seeking. In such cases the traditional view derived from Augustine is that such acts demonstrate the sin of arrogance. However, given the high association of depression and drug abuse with suicide, it is wise to exercise caution in such judgments. Further theological principles include:

> No one ever hates his own body, but he nourishes and tenderly cares for it, just as Christ does for the church, because we are members of his body (Ephesians 5:29–30).

> We do not live to ourselves, and we do not die to ourselves. If we live, we live to the Lord, and if we die, we die to the Lord; so then, whether we live or whether we die, we are the Lord's (Romans 14:7–9).

> Do you not know that your body is a temple of the Holy Spirit within you, which you have from God, and that you are not your own? For you were bought with a price; therefore glorify God in your body (1 Corinthians 6:19–20).

The ultimate painkiller – novocaine for the soul

We are living in the midst of an epidemic, as deadly as the AIDS virus:

- Australia is a world leader, consistently having one of the top three death rates.[2]

- In 1993 there were 1,956 deaths from road accidents, and 2,081 from suicide.

---

1. Victorian Suicide Prevention Task Force Report, July 1997.
2. *The Sydney Morning Herald*, 1996 and Victorian Suicide Prevention Task Force Report, July 1997.

- In 30 years, suicide deaths have doubled for women, and quadrupled for young men.
- Suicide accounts for 3% of all deaths, but 20% of all deaths for 15–24 year olds.
- There are 100,000 suicide attempts each year. This amounts to 30–50 attempts for each male death, and 150–300 attempts for each female death.
- The higher male death rate is due to the use of more lethal methods, like guns.
- The suicide rate is particularly high for young males in rural areas.
- The death of Michael Hutchence in 1997 publicly highlighted the fact that suicide also affects the successful.

In the words of a Counting Crows song:

> ... But the girl in the car in the parking lot says
> 'Man you should try to take a shot, can't you see my walls are crumbling?'
> Then she looks up at the building and says she's thinking of jumping,
> She says she's tired of life: she must be tired of something!
> Round here, she's always on my mind, round here I got lots of time ... [3]

When a young fan took his life, Australian band Silverchair were taken to court over the words of one of their songs, *Suicidal Dream*:

> The people making fun of me, for no reason but jealousy.
> I fantasise about my death, I kill myself from holding my breath.
> My suicidal dream, voices telling me what to do.
> My suicidal dream, I'm sure you will get yours too.
> Help me, comfort me, stop me from feeling what I'm feeling now.
> The rope is here now I'll find a use, I'll kill myself, I'll put my head in the noose.[4]

Our young people are dying like lemmings; dying for a reason to live. Many of them would rather take their own lives than continue to face the pain and hopelessness of modern living. They want to 'eject reality', and when alcohol and drugs fail to blot out the pain, they seek the greatest escapism, the ultimate analgesic – death. After all, in a society where abortion is widely practised, and euthanasia (assisted suicide) was briefly legalised, **why not** take your own life?

---

3. Counting Crows, 'Round Here', *August and Everything After* (Geffen, 1993).
4. Silverchair, 'Suicidal Dream', Frogstomp, Sony Music, 1994.

As the Rev. Tim Costello said recently, 'We are creating a society which will devour its young. It already is'.[5] Dr Germaine Greer has commented, 'It's perfectly reasonable for young people to think they have no future'.[6] What can be done? The focus has begun to move from crisis intervention (the ambulance at the bottom of the cliff), to suicide prevention (the fence at the top of the cliff).

The Victorian Government recently set up a Suicide Prevention Task Force, which reported in July 1997. It commented that:

> It may be that the growing rates of depression and suicidal behaviours reflect ... the increasing presence of social stresses ... prevention is far more effective than intervention. We need to build on and not dismantle our social support structures.[7]

It suggested that key prevention strategies include: strengthening families, creating positive relationships, promoting the role of schools, suicide education for local communities, developing problem solving skills, encouraging sufferers to seek help, and reducing access to the means for attempting suicide.

Current research[8] also indicates that the church has a vital role to play in preventing youth suicide. Yet most members of the church remain unaware there is a problem, let alone that the church has answers to offer. What are the causes of this suicide epidemic, and what hope can the church offer in the face of it?

Cultural changes

One aspect of suicide is a sense of isolation and alienation. Eckersley[9] has identified three aspects of modern culture which reinforce these feelings of existential angst, making the individual more vulnerable (as well as making society less cohesive).

No shared worldview

There is no shared ideal of society and its future, no vision to nurture the individual, and hold society together. Not only have people lost

---

5. Tim Costello quoted in *The Age*.
6. Germaine Greer quoted in *The Age*.
7. Victorian Suicide Prevention Task Force Report, July 1997.
8. See footnotes 9–14.
9. R. Eckersley, 'Values and Visions', *Youth Studies Australia* (Autumn 1995), 15–16.

faith in anything transcending the material world, but belief in material progress itself has now also collapsed.

Moral confusion

Religious and communal values have become individual, secular and material values. Many anti-social vices (pride, greed, lust) have become virtues. Hugh Mackay found:

> young people believe that moral values are declining and (unless they are religious) find it hard to identify an accepted moral code [or to establish] an ethical framework.[10]

Rate of change

The accelerating rate of economic and social change has left us stressed and anxious, on a 'short fuse', where even minor upsets are the last straw.

> It only requires a small spark to ignite feelings of irritation, helplessness, frustration, anger or violence. [We are] trying to cope with too much change, too quickly, and on too many fronts.[11]

Young people lack a clear set of reference points. Without them, people become less resilient, and less resistant to despair. Our culture offers little beyond self-interest to live for, and has failed to provide a sense of meaning and purpose.

Eckersley (who says he is not a Christian) has stated this point another way:

> There is no expectation of an afterlife – no fear of hell, and no hope of heaven – so it doesn't matter if you die.

Robbed of broader, transcendent meaning, many turn inwards to the personal, producing a desperate, pathological obsession

> with our: looks, careers, sex lives, relationships, development, health, fitness ... this makes us more vulnerable to a 'collapse of meaning' when things go wrong in our personal lives.[12]

Our society has failed to heed the warnings of Qoheleth, the preacher,

---

10. H. Mackay, *Young Australians: Attitudes and Values of Today's 10–18 year olds* (Sydney: Mackay Research, 1989), as quoted in Eckersley, 16.
11. H. Mackay, *Reinventing Australia* (Sydney: Angus and Robertson, 1993), 11–20.
12. R. Eckersley, 17.

that such things are 'vanity, and a chasing after the wind' (Ecclesiastes 1:14).

Under pressure

Things **are** going wrong in the personal lives of young people.

- Their parents are the most divorced in history, and this has damaged their self esteem and ability to relate.
- Sexual abuse and homelessness are other aspects of these dysfunctional families, and abuse often precedes a suicide attempt.
- Depression, anxiety and psychiatric problems may affect as many as 15% of teens, and are a factor in 60–90% of suicide attempts.[13]
- Binge drinking and drugs are also used as a means of escape.
- Even anorexia may be an attempt to create meaning by controlling the body.[14]
- Although unemployment averages 8%, youth unemployment is closer to 50% in some areas, with drastic effects on self esteem. No job means no car, no social life and no personal freedom.
- Young people are now being offered 'McJobs', rather than careers, and are the first generation to face a lower standard of living than their parents.
- Those who gain a place at university now have to find the fees.
- Young Australians have had to bear a disproportionate burden as society has undergone enormous social and economic change, a 'second industrial revolution'. If money is the way our society keeps score, then the unemployed and disadvantaged are reduced to being spectators on the sidelines of life.

In the words of an Eels song:

> Life is hard, and so am I
> You'd better give me something so I don't die
> Novocaine for the soul – before I splutter out
> Life is good, and I feel great
> 'Cause Mother says I was a great mistake

---

13. HREOC, 1993, quoted in Eckersley page 18 and footnote 1 above.
14. C. Garrett, *Men and Anorexia Nervosa* (1992), as quoted in Eckersley, 19.

> Novocaine for the soul
> You'd better give me something to fill the hole
> Before I splutter out.[15]

There is an experiment to demonstrate air pressure, where water is boiled inside a drum to drive out the air, then the lid is sealed. This creates a vacuum inside, which cannot withstand the outside air pressure, and the drum soon collapses.

It is not only the cultural changes and personal pressures on young people today that are the problem, it's the spiritual vacuum inside as well. The sense of hopelessness, helplessness and meaninglessness that many young people experience is in fact a spiritual issue. Coming to faith can fill the spiritual vacuum inside, and give a solid core of belief to help withstand the pressures of life.

Church connections

A recent study by Resnick[16] of 36,000 USA high school students measured resiliency by identifying factors which protected students from suicide and other disturbed behaviours, (and seems to offer some empirical support for the original sociological studies of suicide, by Durkheim in 1897[17]).

Resnick's study found a protective function in a perceived sense of caring and connectedness to family, other adults and school. A sense of spirituality, as well as low family stress (which can be caused by poverty, unemployment, substance abuse by parents, domestic violence) also

---

15. The Eels, 'Novocaine for the Soul', from *Beautiful Freak* (MCA Music, 1996).
16. M. Resnick et al, 'The Impact of Caring and Connectedness', *Journal of Paediatrics & Child Health* (1993), 29. The range of behaviours included: absenteeism, dangerous risk taking, delinquency, drug use, pregnancy; and also poor body image, eating disorders, emotional stress, and suicide.
17. E. Durkheim, *Le Suicide*, 1897. Durkheim distinguished three types of suicide, all caused by a disturbance in the relation of society and the individual.
    Egoistic suicide was due to an individual's lack of concern for and involvement in the community, and included suicide due to mental or physical illness and bereavement.
    Altruistic suicide was due to excessive altruism and sense of duty, and included voluntary euthanasia of the elderly, martyrdom, and self-sacrifice in war.
    Anomic suicide was due to the decline or relaxation of social codes such as divorce codes and religious beliefs.
    Egoism and anomie may reinforce each other and lead to a mixed type of suicide, which Resnick's findings seem to confirm, as a sense of belonging to family, school or church is the key factor in resiliency to suicide. Although Freud's psychoanalytic theory is worlds apart from Durkheim, both share a deterministic view of human behaviour, believing that people are subject to powerful forces of which they are not fully aware.

functioned as protective factors. The sense of belonging to family, school or a spirituality was a strong factor in preventing suicide and other high risk behaviours. The study also identified significant relationships with caring adults as being important for youth at risk.

This means the church can play a vital role in suicide prevention. We have 'the words of eternal life' (John 6:68) to offer to an increasingly desperate generation, a gospel which is 'the power of God for salvation to everyone who has faith' (Romans 1:16). Coming to faith can give a shared meaning for life, a moral framework, and a hope for the future. Being connected to a church group can also give a caring community to support young people against the pressures they face. The growing numbers of parish youth workers in Anglican churches are important, as they can be caring adults modelling Christ's love in their relationships with young people.

Theological Insights

A trinitarian perspective on suicide

How can the issue of youth suicide be addressed from a Trinitarian perspective? Before the fall, humanity enjoyed harmony: with God, with others, within themselves, and with creation. The sociological examination above suggests that suicide can be partly understood as an aspect of our fallenness in all four of these areas.

1. In a fallen world, the act of suicide itself is indicative of a profound disharmony with the self (Freud et al), and with creation and society (existential angst, or Durkheim's 'anomie'). Suicide can sometimes seem to be the only answer to the pain and suffering involved in modern life. Illnesses such as depression (linked to suicide in up to 80% of cases), can be seen as one aspect of the disharmony between humanity and self. Reactive depression, provoked by negative circumstances or stress, is a symptom of the disharmony between humanity and creation (as a young person today might express it, 'S--t happens!'), and the disharmony between humanity and society (loneliness, unemployment, abuse).

2. A lack of meaning and purpose in life (Eckersley) is indicative of disharmony with God and his plan. This lack of meaning and purpose is experienced by young people who have no shared world view, who

experience moral confusion and a rapid rate of (mostly negative) social change. This meaninglessness can be seen as a symptom of the disharmony between humanity and creation, and the resulting futility experienced (Romans 8:20–25). It is also a symptom of the disharmony in humanity's relationship with God, and the 'God-shaped gap' which results.

3. A sense of social isolation or not belonging (Durkheim, Resnick) is indicative of a lack of harmony with others. Social belonging is the key factor in resiliency against suicide. The loss of a sense of belonging can be understood as a result of the disharmony with others in society, whether it be loneliness at the individual level, or a sense of alienation from society generally.

The nature of God

My wife was trying to explain the Trinity to our four year old daughter recently, because she's a little confused about how Jesus and God fit together:

> 'Which one is the father, and which one is the son?' my daughter asked. 'God is the father and Jesus is the son,' my wife replied. 'I know they're friends' said my daughter, 'because they've got the same haircut!'

The Trinity indicates that relationships lie at the heart of reality, because they are present in the very nature of God. Relationships within the Trinity commenced before creation, and are eternal, being part of God's very nature. Before anything else was created, God's moral character could only be expressed as the persons of the Trinity related to each other. God is a God of relationship, because God enjoys relationship within himself.

If God is personal and relational, then his self-revelation is a natural consequence. He reveals himself through his Word in order to enter into relationship with his creatures. We are invited to share in the bond of unity the Father, Son and Holy Spirit enjoy. God is Love, and takes the initiative to create a relationship of love with us. This love is epitomised by the sacrifice of the Cross, which is also the act which makes entry into this new relationship with God possible.

> The scriptural basis for Christian belief in the triune God is not the scanty Trinitarian formulas of the New Testament, but...the cross; and the shortest

expression of the Trinity is the divine act of the cross, in which the Father allows the Son to sacrifice himself through the Spirit.[18]

Jesus came to restore harmony in our relationship with God, harmony in our social relationships (through creating God's new society where people are in true relationship with each other and God), and harmony in our relationship within our selves, by restoring our true humanity in his image. Through his death on the cross, Jesus has made it possible for these relationships to be restored.

Christ's suffering and ours

The place to start considering a Trinitarian theology therefore, is the Cross itself. 'The grace of our Lord Jesus Christ' is epitomised by his sacrificial death on the cross, and the suffering he endured also means he understands the suffering which often drives people to suicide. What comfort does the 'God forsaken God' hanging on the cross have to offer to suffering young people? According to Moltmann,[19] anyone who suffers thinks at first he has been forsaken by God; but anyone who cries out to God in this suffering echoes the death-cry of the dying Christ. God becomes not someone set over against him, but the human God who cries with him and intercedes for him with his Cross. Suffering is part of living and loving, because the one who loves becomes vulnerable to hurt and disappointment. We live because we love, and we suffer because we love. How can one continue to love despite grief, death, or disappointment? In the faith which springs from the Cross we know that when we suffer, Christ suffers in us.

The Fatherless Son

'The love of God the Father' is epitomised by his willingness to sacrifice his only Son for our sakes. God the Father suffered bereavement when his Son died, and they were separated for the first time in eternity. What comfort can the bereaved Father offer to the families of suicide victims? As Moltmann[20] also notes, the Cross divides the Father from the Son 'to the utmost degree of enmity and distinction'. The first person of the Trinity casts out and annihilates the second. 'He who did not withhold his own Son, but gave him up for all

---

18. B. Steffen, *The Dogma of the Cross,* in J. Moltmann, *The Crucified God,* (New York: Harper & Row, 1974), 241.
19. Moltmann, 252.
20. Moltmann, 152, 241ff.

of us, will he not with him also give us everything else?' (Romans 8:32). God casts out and delivers up his own Son to an accursed death. Paul says even more clearly Christ became 'a curse for us' (Galatians 3:13) and 'for our sake he made him to be sin' (2 Corinthians 5:21). God delivers up the Son for godless and 'godforsaken' humanity. Because God does not spare his own Son all the godless are spared. They are not Godforsaken, precisely because God has abandoned his own Son for them, which is the basis for the justification of the godless.

The Sonless Father

Moltmann[21] goes on to observe that in the surrender of the Son, the Father also surrenders himself, though not in the same way. The Father suffers the death of the Son in the infinite grief of love. To understand the Cross, it is necessary to talk in Trinitarian terms (and to avoid the dangers of patripassianism, which claimed the Father also suffered and died, or of theopaschitism, which spoke of the 'death of God' in Christ's death). The Son suffers dying, while the Father suffers the death of the Son, and the grief of the Father is just as important as the death of the Son. The Fatherlessness of the Son is matched by the Sonlessness of the Father, and he suffers the death of his Fatherhood in the death of the Son. He has suffered the death of Jesus and shown the force of his love, and in him we can also find the power to continue to love.

The Bible speaks of both the Father delivering up the Son and of the Son delivering up himself. The 'deliver up' formula occurs in Paul with both the Father and Son as subject: 'the Son of God, who loved me and gave himself for me' (Galatians 2:20, compare Romans 8:32). This emphasises the deep conformity between the will of the Father and the Son in the Cross event, as the Gethsemane narrative also records. John 3:16 sums this up, and emphasises that nowhere is this love seen more clearly than in the event of the Cross.

The strong link between depression and suicide raises the issue of sickness and death as consequences of the fall. Once again God's answer is found in the Cross, because the purpose of Jesus' death was to conquer sickness, suffering and death. His resurrection was God's declaration that through Jesus there is a new possibility of life, and it

---

21. Moltmann, 243ff.

also points forward to his perfect world, where there will be no more mourning, pain or death (Revelation 21). God also gives us resources to cope with illness through his Spirit and his Church, and gives a hope in Him that sickness can never take away.

Meaning and purpose

Today there is no common worldview, and metanarratives such as the Bible are no longer endorsed by the majority of society. Many today see life as meaningless and without purpose. A Trinitarian theology offers a strong explanation for the lack of meaning and purpose in modern life. Creation has been thrown out of balance by the Fall, and the lack of harmony between humanity and God, self, others, and nature is the cause of the futility, frustration and meaninglessness of modern life (Ephesians 4:17).

As well as offering an explanation for the problem, the Bible also offers a solution. To believe in God's plan was to see history as a salvation-history, which explained the past, the present and the future to come; and to see the Cross of Christ as the turning point of history. The Christian faith provided a shared metanarrative or worldview, which was teleological in nature. A world without a knowledge of God, his plan, and the Cross is a world without meaning and purpose.

Because humanity is created in the image of a relational God, we are also made for relationships. Our desire for belonging, love and acceptance come from being made in God's image, and made for a relationship with him. Our primary relational need is for a renewed relationship with our Creator. The words of Augustine might have been written for this restless generation, 'You have made us for yourself, and our hearts are restless till they find their rest in you'.[22]

Pascal also spoke of this reality when he spoke of the 'God-shaped gap' in every person,[23] or as Ecclesiastes says, 'He has also set eternity in the hearts of men' (Ecclesiastes 3:11 NIV).

Without hope and meaning in life, the future is bleak and we stare death in the eyes. In such a situation, alcohol and drugs can be a way of escape. 'If the dead are not raised, "Let us eat and drink, for tomorrow we die." ' said Paul (1 Corinthians 15:32).

---

22. St Augustine, *Confessions* (Middlesex, England: Penguin, 1961), 21
23. B. Pascal, *Pensées* (Middlesex, England: Penguin, 1968), 75.

But he also wrote:

> But in fact Christ has been raised from the dead, the first fruits of those who have died. For ... the resurrection of the dead has also come through a human being ... all will be made alive in Christ (1 Corinthians 15:20–22).

Christ's death and resurrection form the hinge point of history. We need to tell young people that because of Christ's death, resurrection, and his promised return there is hope and meaning for the future. The Eels song is right to look to Christ for the answer:

> Life is white, and I am black
> Jesus and his lawyer are coming back
> Oh my darling, will you be here?
> Before I splutter out.[24]

The church as community

We are also created for social relationships. Even though God himself was there with Adam in Eden, he still said 'it is not good that the man should be alone', and created woman to be with him (Genesis 2:18). Humans are created as social creatures who desire relationship. When we are deprived of relationship we experience loneliness, because we were never created to be alone. Our fear of loneliness and alienation is the fear of something unbearable to our natures, because we are made for relationships with each other.

> When your day is night alone, and you feel like letting go
> If you think you've had too much of this life – well hang on
> Cause everybody hurts, take comfort in a friend
> Everybody hurts ...
> Don't throw in your hand, oh no, don't throw in your hand
> And you feel like you're alone – no, no, no, you're not alone![25]

Loneliness and a sense of abandonment (rather than belonging) are factors in suicide which often lead to despair. Through his death on the Cross, Jesus experienced separation from his Father to spare us from forsakenness and loneliness. Now through his church, a new community is being created for us to belong to. 'The fellowship of the Holy Spirit' is expressed on earth through the Body of Christ, the community of the Church, which needs to mirror the intimacy of relationships experienced by the persons of the Trinity.

---

24. The Eels, 'Novocaine for the Soul' from *Beautiful Freak* (MCA Music, 1996).
25. R.E.M., 'Everybody Hurts', from *Automatic for the People* (Warner Brothers, 1992).

The new community created through the Spirit is seen in Acts 2:42–47 and Acts 4:32–35, and had a powerful witness which attracted others: 'having the goodwill of all the people. And day by day the Lord added to their number those who were being saved' (Acts 2:47). This community was able to reach out to others, and 'there was not a needy person among them' because 'all who believed were together and had all things in common' (Acts 4:34; 2:44). As well as material care, the early church also offered supportive caring relationships, as seen in the 'one another' statements of the New Testament:

> We are members one of another (Romans 12:5).
>
> Love one another with mutual affection (Romans 12:10)
>
> Outdo one another in showing honour (Romans 12:10).
>
> Welcome one another, therefore, just as Christ has welcomed you (Romans 15:7).
>
> … the members may have the same care for one another (1 Corinthians 12:25).
>
> Through love become slaves to one another (Galatians 5:13).
>
> Bear one another's burdens (Galatians 6:2).
>
> Bearing with one another in love … (Ephesians 4:2).
>
> Be subject to one another out of reverence for Christ (Ephesians 5:21).
>
> Forgive each other; just as the Lord has forgiven you (Colossians 3:13).
>
> Teach and admonish one another in all wisdom (Colossians 3:16).
>
> Confess your sins to one another (James 5:16).
>
> Pray for one another (James 5:16).
>
> Exhort one another every day (Hebrews 3:13).
>
> Encourage one another and build up each other (1 Thessalonians 5:11).
>
> Love one another (John 13:34).

The Church is God's new community, where all are included (Ephesians 2:14–15), and this community can reach out to the isolated and lonely and offer them a supportive and accepting family, a place to belong, and people who can love them with the love of Christ. The quality of relationships in the church community is supposed to be a foretaste of heaven.

In the land of the absent father, the church can also become a surrogate family, where God can re-parent individuals through relationships with his people. The church is a place of refuge and hope for those from dysfunctional families. Youth ministers and youth leaders can also be significant adults for young people, modelling Christ's love in their relationships with young people ('Speak … to younger men as brothers … to younger women as sisters – with absolute purity', 1 Timothy 5:1–2). As young people enter into community, they can also discover who they are and what gifts they have to offer, and recapture the image of God as they seek to become mature and Christlike.

Conclusion

Resnick (and Durkheim) quoted previously, seem to agree that it is not so much the content of the Christian faith that helps to prevent suicide, but the sense of social belonging found in a church. However, even if a desire to belong is the presenting need motivating young people, most Christian leaders would suggest that the deeper (but often unfelt) need is ultimately a spiritual one.

Even if young people join the church initially for friendship (an associational faith), they may go on to enter into a personal relationship with God as the gospel is proclaimed, and their deepest spiritual needs are addressed, finding a meaning and purpose to life as a result. This is why ministries of the Word, through evangelism and teaching, should always be a foundational part of our youth ministry.

In this way, the church can play a preventative role in youth suicide, as it offers not only somewhere for young people to belong, but the answer to their deepest spiritual need: meaning and purpose through a relationship with their Creator and Redeemer. Ultimately, it is only the gospel that can offer an answer to the search for meaning in life, by restoring relationship with the Author of life; and it is only membership in the body of Christ that can answer the search for belonging, by restoring an individual to God and his people.

CHAPTER TEN

You are what you are called:
Trinity, self and vocation
Gordon Preece

Introduction
My tall task in this paper is to unpack the three realities described in the title: youth identity, vocational calling and the doctrine of the Trinity. God calls in a threefold way, as Father, Son and Spirit fulfil their varied vocations in the history of humanity and the economy of salvation in complete unity. This overflows into our life, calling us to see our identity (self), intimacy (relationships) and industry (work) in the light of God's triune nature and work with integrity (integration). The paper will look:

1. at the fragmented sense of self or identity in hyper- or postmodernity where there is little time or space for youth, or a coherent sense of identity; before

2. setting identity in the light of the Trinity; and then

3. seeing a sense of self as vocation in response to God's threefold call.

Shifting, fragmented senses of postmodern selves
This paper emerges out of a personal and pastoral struggle to understand my own identity and that of those to whom I minister as a former youth worker and pastor, now ethics teacher and father of two teens and one 'wannabe' teen. In my search I found help from philosophical, sociological, psychological and especially theological sources.

Philosophical and sociological perspectives on the split self
Young people are caught in a series of philosophical and sociological tug-of-wars over identity in our society. Robert Bellah's *Habits of the*

Heart notes a split between Monday's more 'modern' economic individualism (the public, working or role self) using an economic rationalist, utilitarian or cost-benefit calculation of pleasure over pain; and Sunday's more postmodern expressive or therapeutic individualism of the heart (the personal, intimate, creative, emotional or real self in family, nature and free time). The first sees itself as realistic, the second as Romantic.[1]

The film *Dead Poet's Society* made by Australian director Peter Weir illustrates this clash. The young hero, Neil, preferred suicide to a parental ban on his ambition to be an actor. His father, a lawyer and economic individualist (old middle class), had sweated and saved to send him to a top college so that he could enter a respectable and lucrative profession like medicine. But his son placed a higher value on creativity and individual expression (new middle class). The reception the film received showed that Neil is not the only one – many people identified with him.[2]

John Naisbitt's *Megatrends* sees us split between technological developments or high-tech (Monday) and human development or high-touch (Sunday).[3] Sherry Terkle[4] chronicles the movement towards virtual high-tech selves in the computer age, a particular preoccupation of many young people who are the generational guinea pigs of this technology. She finds them using this high technology to make new microworlds to mirror back to themselves their emotions and identity, or their hi-touch expressive side.

Psychological perspectives on the shifting self

Among the mass of contemporary psychological theorists addressing identity or self issues are Cushman, Mitchell, Seligman, Colapietro,

---

1. This is in the sense of the 19th century naturalistic and literary reaction to Industrialism and rationalism.
2. Compare Cat Stevens' song *Father and Son*. The father says 'work hard boy, you'll find, one day you'll have a job like mine, job like mine', to which the son replies, 'but I know, for sure, nobody should be that poor.' Cat Stevens' eventually found in Islam the riches he was looking for that he couldn't find in Greek Orthodoxy. In *Saturday Night Fever* John Travolta works in a boring role in a hardware store but comes alive as an expressive self by dancing on Saturday nights.
3. At the time of TV's introduction, encounter groups mushroomed. During the age of computers and high-tech medicine, New Age thinking, holistic medicine and ecological awareness have flourished.
4. S. Terkle, *The Second Self: Computers and the Human Spirit* (London: Granada, 1984), especially Chapter 4 'Adolescence and Identity: Finding Yourself in the Machine'.

Gergen and Lifton.[5] Philip Cushman examines the contemporary shift from the Victorian sexually and monetarily restricted 'bounded, masterful self', to the post-World War II empty self. This 'self ... experiences a significant absence of community, tradition, and shared meaning ... being continually filled up by consuming goods, calories, experiences, politicians, romantic partners and empathetic therapists ... to combat the growing alienation and fragmentation of its era'. He accuses the state, advertising and the self-improvement industry of perpetuating and profiting from 'the ideology of the empty self' – as do individualistic, therapeutic Church and youth groups.[6]

There is a broad consensus that the self in the last two millennia has increasingly become more individualistic, subjective and deeper.[7] The 19th century Romantic notion of unique 'personality' links in with this, and with various Christian forms:[8] Evangelical pietism – with its stress on heart religion; Anglo-Catholicism, emphasising beauty, ritual, mysticism and tradition (compare Taize youth services); and charismatics accenting the divine and human spirit and experience.

Further, the very notion of adolescence as a time of identity crisis, and discovering personality, may be a post-industrial historical construction, arising from the shifting of adolescents from productive to consumptive roles (to sell CDs and Levis) – not a natural law as so many Christian manuals on raising teens assume. In fact, we could argue for abolishing adolescence as an historical anachronism.

Martin Seligman argues that because our society promotes a pathological form of selfhood 'whose pleasures and pains ... successes and failures occupy centre stage in our society', depression is on the increase. This over-ambitious self almost inevitably sets itself up for a fall.[9] Its individualism is a fair weather philosophy. It has no umbrella when the rain falls on the just and unjust. Without faith and hope in

---

5. Compare also Roy Porter ed., *Rewriting the Self: Histories from the Renaissance to the Present* (London and New York: Routledge, 1997).
6. P. Cushman, 'Why the Self is Empty: Toward a Historically Situated Psychology', *American Psychologist*, Vol. 45, No. 5 (May 1990), 608. Compare his *Constructing the Self, Constructing America: A Cultural History of Psychotherapy*, (Reading, Massachusetts: Addison-Wesley, 1995).
7. See Charles Taylor, *Sources of the Self* (Cambridge, Massachusetts: Harvard University Press, 1989).
8. See Lesslie Newbigin, *The Other Side of 1984*, WCC, (Geneva, 1984), 13, and David Bebbington, Ridley College Lectures, 1997.
9. M. Seligman, 'Boomer Blues', *Psychology Today*, (October, 1988).

the larger 'benevolent' institutions of Church, family or nation, or vocational roles mediating between us and the cosmos, which were used as an umbrella in the past, we now interpret personal loss or failure, such as unemployment, as catastrophic. We have no 'buffer zone' between us and the abyss of self-annihilation or Durkheim's *anomie* leading to suicide.

Australian youth consultant Richard Eckersley echoes this, arguing that young countries like Australia, the US and New Zealand have high rates of youth suicide because of the lack of longer and larger traditions or narratives of meaning, which young people can draw on in hard times or when facing the despair of ecological or economic disaster.[10]

Further, the very notion of a stable self is under siege. Psychoanalyst Stephen A. Mitchell sees two main post-Freudian perspectives on the self – 'the self as relational, multiple, and discontinuous ... and the self as separate from others, integral, and continuous'.[11] Vincent M. Colapietro outlines the even more radical deconstructionist approaches to the self. They are variations on Nietzsche's philosophical fatherhood of postmodernity: 'And as for the ego! It has become a fable, a fiction, a play on words: it has totally ceased to think, to feel, and to will'. The father of deconstructionism, Jacques Derrida, attacks our 'everyday presumptions of identity, intention, and legal status'. The 'I' is a mere fiction generated by a linguistic 'play of differences' – an 'anonymous multiplicity'.[12] This celebration of difference, ambiguity and multiplicity – the self as a language game or mere cipher for culture and power – is common. Robert J. Lifton's *The Protean Self* draws on the image of the Greek god Proteus, who constantly changes shape and size, as the patron saint or divinity of postmodernity's constantly changing chameleon self. He sees this changing self as a resource for 'human resilience in an age of fragmentation'.[13] Musicians like David Bowie, Madonna, Kylie and Danni Minogue with their multiple incarnations and images, reflect, as well as help create, this trend.

Multiple identities and images also increase turnover of CDs, clothes

---

10. Paper delivered at the Combined Churches Conference on Ecology, Eastwood, 1990.
11. S.A. Mitchell, 'Contemporary Perceptions on Self: Toward an Integration', *Psychoanalytic Dialogues*, I/2 (1991), 126.
12. V.M. Colapietro, 'The Integral Self: Systematic Illusion or Inescapable Task?', *Listening: Journal of Culture and Religion*, Vol. 25, No. 3, (Fall, 1990), 195.
13. *The Protean Self: Human Resilience in an Age of Fragmentation*, (New York: Basic Books, 1993).

and above all, capital, for postmodernity has a material and technological as well as linguistic basis. Kenneth J. Gergen shows how powerful new technologies like faxes, computers, email and the web, vastly increase our exposure to relationships and alternate lifestyles and possible selves. They speed up the process of identity formation through significant and insignificant others.[14] This is why I see postmodernity as hyper- or fractured modernity.[15]

This technological trend has great potential but is particularly dangerous for younger people exposed to hi-tech without the hi-touch of stable long-term relationships from which to draw identity. Consequently they can become more and more like Legion – the Gadarene demoniac (Mark 5:1–20). In the movies *Chasing Amy* and *The Ice Storm*, younger people from fractured or fracturing families struggle to find any stable sense of self or relationship (opting in the former to fantasise through comics). Commitment does not come easily to them. The postmodern motto could well be 'stable relationships are for horses!'

Post/hypermodern deconstructionism, and the 'discontinuity' school of psychoanalysis have rightly questioned the historically dominant Greek or Platonic view of the self as more stable and static than it is. The self is not set in the concrete of a Greek metaphysics of eternal forms. But, Colapietro perceptively asks,

> can a radically decentred and irreducibly heteronomous 'self', can 'an anonymous multiplicity' say 'No' in a manner and for the duration required for effective opposition? Without an integral self, can there be any genuine possibility of resistance to oppression or exploitation?[16]

The deconstructionist critique of integral selfhood 'common to Greek metaphysics, Christian theology, and Enlightenment rationality' may in fact undermine liberal democracy by developing people incapable of trust or keeping promises. Is this what comes from abandoning an

---

14. K.J. Gergen, *The Saturated Self: Dilemmas of Identity in Contemporary Life* (New York: Basic Books, 1991).
15. Drawing particularly on English materialist and sociological analyses of postmodernity, for example, David Harvey, *The Condition of Postmodernity* (Oxford: Blackwell, 1990), and Anthony Giddens, *The Consequences of Modernity*, (California: Stanford University Press, 1990).
16. Colapietro, *Integral Self*, 195.

ahistorical natural centre, and replacing it with a perception of the self as a 'centreless web of historically conditioned beliefs and desires'?[17]

Charlene Spretnak resists the modern 'socially engineered' mechanistic and atomistic self, which has nature as mere 'background matter' and the body as subject to strong rational control. She also rejects the deconstructionist postmodern 'wordy' view that we are mere fragmented selves or language machines in a socially constructed or virtual reality with erasable bodies. Instead she proposes an 'ecological postmodern' 'self in process' in all its trustworthy embodiedness, ecological earthiness and holistic web-like character in a network of relationships where family, neighbourhood, bio-region, nation, earth, cosmos 'are the extended boundaries of the self' and 'god' is seen as 'creativity in the cosmos'.[18] This may move in the right direction, but is still not far enough, as it doesn't include the Trinitarian God, who is both transcendent and immanent, who creates and moves within the cosmos and our very selves.

Privatising time and space for youth

Increasingly, an economically rationalist or fundamentalist society has little time or space for young people, except as consumers and consumer products. Youth is an increasingly extended period of non-productivity due to prolonged education and unemployment. Rebellion is no longer expressed in the modern way by moving away, because it is often not economically possible, and the government's youth and unemployment allowances tie teens and even twenty-somethings economically to their parents.

As John Ryan argues: 'If older people [like Melbourne Catholic Monsignor Peter Elliott, episcopal vicar for religious education and critic of grunge] don't understand the disillusionment of young kids, it's because they had free education, job certainty and economic independence by their mid-20s'. This raises real issues of generational justice. Modern progress has become a myth to teens. They feel like they bear much of the risk of living in a 'risk society',[19] where everyone

---

17. Colapietro, *Integral Self*, 196, 202.
18. C. Spretnak, *The Resurgence of the Real: Body, Nature and Place in a Hypermodern World* (Reading, Massachusetts: Addison-Wesley, 1997), 72–73.
19. Sociologists Ulrich Beck and Anthony Giddens' term to describe postmodernity.

has to be an entrepreneur selling themselves, and if they fail it's their fault: user pays.

Adolescence (and Gen X and postmodernity) itself is in many ways a consumer creation, a product of market segmentation defining adolescents against adults (producers) in an adversarial and fragmenting way. Increasingly, adolescents are defined against each other in terms of various consumer lifestyles such as grunge, gothic (in which Anglicans are specialists!), skateboard and homeboy, or Coburg black Adidas tracksuit styles. Grunge may be seen as expressing teen frustration, anger, 'dissatisfaction with economic excess' (op-shop jumpers and unkempt hair as trademarks),[20] but it soon, like the hippie movement, gets co-opted commercially.

Public space for young people is increasingly being privatised. The lack of youth space is particularly seen in the tendency to criminalise youth: through neighbourhood watch, negative media portrayals, city, tram, nightclub and shopping centre surveillance, maulings by security guards of 'undesirable youths' hanging round in the private space of shopping centres, banning skateboarding in cities and so on. Grim media tales of a youth crime epidemic criminalise them as a class and rarely mention the destructive context for many young people.

> Mass unemployment, the dismantling of public welfare, educational, transport and health services, exploitative and inequitable youth wage structures, government rule by decree, and ... a competitive casino culture all underpin the experience of youth ... Social indicators show ... young people over-represented among the unemployed, the poor, those who commit suicide, and road deaths. The problems experienced by a growing proportion of young people – to make ends meet, to find secure full-time employment, to cope with stress and educational competition, to forge a meaningful social identity – are nevertheless construed ... to make young people themselves 'the problems'.[21]

At the same time private or personal space and time is being taken over by work time and space, as two-income families no longer have time

---

20. 'Grunge versus God', *The Age* (11 February 1998), Opinion. Contrast Monsignor P. Elliott, 'Church Youth are Rebels with a Cause' on the same page. Also see Hugh Mackay, *Generations* (Sydney: Angus & Robertson, 1997) on the way the goal posts have moved.
21. Rob White, Associate Professor of Criminology, University of Melbourne, 'Some facts behind the figures of the young people's "crime wave" ', *The Age* (11 December, 1997), A11. Compare the construal of Aboriginal people.

for younger people (even to teach them to speak, according to some speech pathologists). They use industrial concepts like planned quality time[22] to cut down on the time and space needed for genuinely spontaneous and indirect side by side communication (such as driving together).

In the fallout from the nuclear family catastrophe (this generation are the physical, if not spiritual, survivors of huge levels of abortion and divorce), the absence of parental guidance, particularly marked in the movie *Kids*,[23] leads to either anarchic behaviour or surveillance by Big Brother. Substitute families such as gangs form, and peer groups and mates can exert frightening corporate power that leads to the collapse of individuality into a herd or crowd mentality. This is seen in the Australian teen movie *Blackrock* where a powerful peer leader who turns rapist and murderer exerts power over another young man, whose father has abdicated all responsibility and whose mother struggles with her resentful son and her own breast cancer.

Christians who worship their 'sacred' families and youth groups, who have a defensive view of their space, are no different to non-Christians building bigger walls or moats around their castles (note the title of the recent Australian movie *The Castle*), raising the drawbridge and establishing Anglo-Saxon middle-class 'lifestyle enclaves'. They need to heed the story Jim Wallis told us on his 1995 Australian visit of two young gang members shooting it out on the street – the one on the receiving end ran into a church for sanctuary, but it failed to stop the other. Sub-machine gun bullets riddled the church in the midst of a service. The next day church leaders publicly condemned this blasphemous violation of 'sacred space', but a black street preacher had the final word: 'If you don't take the church to the streets, the streets will come to the church'.

The same applies in Australia. Recently a clergy friend was in St Paul's Cathedral, Melbourne when he saw two shadowy figures near the pulpit and went closer to investigate. Through the gloom he saw a

---

22. See Arlie Russel Hochschild, *The Time Bind: When Work Becomes Home and Home Becomes Work* (New York: Metropolitan Books, 1997).
23. Compare Naomi Wolf's *(Promiscuities: A Secret History of Female Desire*, Chatto & Windus, 1997, 19, 25–26) personal account of the San Francisco 70s generation's virtual abandonment of their children to precocious sexuality without appropriate guidance or initiation. 'Children ... were peripheral to the adults' playtime. Sometimes it seemed as though everyone was a child'.

young couple having sex. By this time he'd disturbed them, and after a discussion he found out they'd just met that morning at Flinders St Station. They got their clothes on and went their not so merry way, while my friend asked a cathedral attendant what the cathedral was doing about these kids. He was told they'd just bought a new $60,000 security system! Imagine what sort of youth work you could do there with that money. What do these two incidents and what does the Trinitarian God, who makes time and space for young people, say to the Church and to Melbourne Anglicans, with a Cathedral right opposite the homeless street kids of Flinders St Station? Fortunately there are some like the Cathedral verger and Shirley Osborne and her family who make time and space. Shirley started Steps ministry to homeless youth while breastfeeding her baby on the station steps, and has since had hundreds through her home.

The triune God makes time, space and gives us a voice

Divine indwelling as making hospitable time and space

Against a modern deistic, detached view of God, for which vocation and identity acted like a vice holding people in place in a static career and social order, we need a way to reconstitute a stable self that is dynamic. We need to draw on the Trinitarian notion of divine 'selves' or persons in relation and history; a God who makes time and space and gives voice to humanity, and in particular youth, when few others do.

The idea of divine indwelling, that is 'the Father is in me and I am in the Father' (John 10:38; compare 14:10-11, 17:21, 7:16), or *perichoresis* means 'making room'. In the mutual relationships of the Trinity each makes room for the other in non-possessive ways. Their identity does not dissolve in the relationship as is the tendency in some teen peer groups, but neither is it 'self-enclosed' and isolated. The Trinitarian persons are not defined oppositionally to the others, like teens reacting against parents. 'The boundaries of the self are porous and shifting', dotted not solid lines. They are open to other and the different as enriching, not threatening the self, a contrast to conformist peer and Christian groups maintained by strong boundaries rather than a strong centre. In this sense each person of the Trinity has a 'catholic personality' open to others.[24]

This divine openness to others overflows to the church and humanity through Christ's and the Spirit's indwelling us. Jesus says 'I will not leave you orphaned' (John14:12–20). 'I am in my Father, and you in me, and I in you.' And through this mutual indwelling the world comes to believe too (John 17:21). It is an act of hospitality, of making time and space in oneself for others, making them at home, something many younger people have little experience of, even at the level of sitting down to a family meal together without the TV being on.

Dangers of monologues or one-handedness

God is not a monologue, lecturing in the way teens hate parents doing (anything longer than one sentence!). Instead God openly invites or calls us into dialogue, allowing us to voice our concerns, and Jesus and the Spirit to voice them for us. God is engaged in an eternal, inviting conversation calling us into being and giving us voice out of that conversation in Word and Spirit. Allowing youth their voice is grounded in God's Trinitarian character as a dialogue – or better trialogue – a process of open, equal communication or calling of each other to fulfil their unique vocation for the world.

This Trinitarian communication model is very different to what Mark Davis calls the *Gangland*[25] of Australian literary and pop culture, which effectively keeps younger writers, musicians and cultural forms from having their say and entering into the inner circles of the Baby Boomers, where decisions are made as to who will be heard or get airplay. The mainstream media, according to Davis, trivialise or demonise young people's beliefs, actions, heroes, speech and tastes. Whether he is right or not, it often feels that way to young people, and so functions as a sociological fact.

The church, apart from Archbishop Rayner's dialogue with two young people in his 1997 Advent conversations, has likewise often

---

24. Miroslav Volf, ' "The Trinity is our Social Program" – the Doctrine of the Trinity and the Shape of Social Engagement', *Modern Theology*, Vol 14, No. 3, (July 1998), 403–423. Compare J. Zizioulas, *Being as Communion: Studies in Personhood and the Church*, (Crestwood, NY: St Vladimir's Seminary Press, 1985). We could also say that the Social Trinity is our youth program.
25. M. Davis, *Gangland* (St Leonards, NSW: Allen & Unwin, 1997).

'monologued' to young people. Theologically, this reflects a kind of Trinitarian subordinationism, as if one (older) person has more right to speak than another. But both Word and Spirit (breath) equally proceed from the one 'mouth' of God even though they are often (like young people) not given equal voice.

Another helpful Trinitarian image is from the second century Church Father Irenaeus, who spoke of God as a worker creating and redeeming the world using two hands – the Word and the Spirit. Sadly many churches and youth groups are one handed, or unitarian, having amputated or under-used their other hand. We focus on one person or article of the Creed to the neglect of the others.[26] This leads to some short-term practical strengths, but has long-term weaknesses and imbalances. We need to become ambidextrous again.

The Father's antidote to cosmic orphanhood and voicelessness

A focus on God as Creator or Father has great strengths, but also weaknesses where the Australian and modern workaholic distortion of absentee or abusive human fathers is projected onto God and isolated from Jesus' style of sonship. Australians, especially young Australians, suffer from 'A Case of Cosmic Orphanhood'[27] or 'underfathering'. Associate Professor Michael Carr-Gregg of Melbourne's Centre for Adolescent Health advocates role models such as the Robin Williams character, Mr Keating in *Dead Poets Society* for many

> 'underfathered' young boys because the only men they came into contact with at school were the caretaker and the principal – perpetuating the notion that 'men are only good for building and bossing' … Many boys are emotionally

---

26. As H. Richard Niebuhr argues in 'An Attempt at a Theological Analysis of the Church's Missionary Motivation', *Occasional Bulletin from the Missionary Research Library*, New York, 14. 1 (1963): 1-6 and 'The Doctrine of the Trinity and the Unity of the Church', *Theology Today* (October 1946 and July 1983), 371–384. Compare Richard Mouw, *The God Who Commands* (University of Notre Dame Press, 1990), Chapter 8, 'The Triune Commander'.
27. John Smith, *Advance Australia Where?* (Homebush West: Anzea, 1988), Chapter 2. Compare David Blenkinsopp, *Fatherless America: Confronting Our Most Urgent Social Problem* (New York: Basic Books, 1995).

atrophied – they're spiritual anorexics who don't believe in themselves let alone anyone else. They don't know how to communicate.[28]

The teenage boys of *Dead Poets Society* were only able to express themselves as individuals, reading the Romantic love poets and acting, because they were mentored into a society – romantic individualism is not enough.

A lot of youth work involves a form of re-parenting (like pioneer Anglican youth worker John Kidson did for many young men at French's Forest and still in Lismore), particularly as stable, middle class, modern families are under threat in postmodernity. Premature exposure to adult experience leaves young people in a state of being orphaned, open game in a market society. This is a reason to provide long-term and more secure youth work for many teens suffering the effects of family failure and the transience of postmodern relationships. (I speak from experience, both my youth work jobs were terminated in under a year.) However the vocational insecurity of youth work does help you identify with young people!

Divine fathering/parenting is just as important for young women. Church historian Roberta Bondi[29] came from a broken family – her father walked out in her teens. She had always found him difficult to approach or disagree with. For many years this affected her view of God's fatherhood, until she found through the desert fathers that the Johannine Jesus said 'I and the Father are one'. She then saw the way Mary and Martha questioned and challenged Jesus without rebuke concerning their brother Lazarus' death in John 11. Then she realised that if Jesus and the Father are one, God is like that too, a father who allows his adolescent children their voice, calling them into adulthood. In this way, autonomy, a classic adolescent virtue, is given its relative place, relative to relationships, but not turned into an absolute.

God's non-patriarchal Fatherhood is a helpful and challenging model for youth workers and for me as a parent of teens. Eugene Peterson

---

28. In response to a recent Victorian study showing many 17–21 year old boys had harsh, sexist attitudes about women and sex, for example that drunk and provocatively dressed young women were ripe for rape. 'Boys are Learning to Live and Love,' *The Age* (28 February 1998). Compare Steven Biddulph's book *Raising Boys*, (Lane Cove: Finch, 1997) where he says that if you are working 60 hours a week including commuting you just won't cut it as a Dad.
29. Roberta C. Bondi, 'Be Not Afraid: Praying to God the Father', *Modern Theology* 9, 3 July 1993, 235ff.

says[30] you think that now you're physically fully grown (at least vertically!), secure career wise, and have your own home, you can settle down securely – with no need for further personal and spiritual growth. Then along comes this gangling, unsettled, challenging teenager who is growing in all directions and demands that you continue to grow too. Jesus and God the Father are not afraid of that kind of growth. Neither should we be.

Jesus as God's Son and our elder brother

It is not only a renewed sense of divine fatherhood that we need but a new sense of Jesus as God's unique Son, our Creator and elder brother, 'the first born over all creation' (Colossians 1:15; compare verse 19 and Hebrews 2:11). This was of great significance to me as a tormented, teary teenager, isolated from my peers as I went through my own sort of nervous breakdown while my mother went through two of her own (including receiving shock treatment). It also compensated me for the loss of my elder brother Guy, who died on my birth date exactly one year before I was born.

This Christlike role of elder brother has been played for me by older peers, youth leaders and mentors at various life stages, initiating me into the next stage in my Christian journey. But it is particularly important at the youth stage, when teens are distancing themselves from their own parents and their parents' faith according to the prepared script of our society, but needing other models of faith. I am fortunate that my kids can identify with other Christian models at Ridley College, but in many ways they have been under-discipled in Melbourne Diocese compared with what I received as a youth in Sydney.

The Spirit as the forgotten or isolated member of the Trinity

To have a fully biblical and Trinitarian credal view of our identity and vocation we also need to do more justice to the role of the Holy Spirit than most Anglican churches do. We are often like Monsignor Quixote in Graeme Greene's book of that title. In trying to explain the Trinity to his communist mayor friend he pours three glasses of whisky, one for

---

30. E. Peterson, *Like Dew Your Youth: Growing Up with Your Teenager*, (Grand Rapids: Eerdmans, 1994), 7–9.

the Father, one for the Son, but only has enough for a half glass for the Spirit.

Many evangelicals in practice subordinate the Spirit to the Word or Christ while many Anglo Catholics subordinate the Spirit to the Church or sacraments. Charismatics or Pentecostals on the other hand can undiscerningly separate the Spirit from Christ, while others separate the Spirit from God as Creator, thus confining the Spirit to the Church and focusing only on supernatural gifts in the church. Liberals however, often connect the Spirit to creation, but not Christ, leading to an acceptance of all experience as leadings or words of the Spirit today, for example the homosexual feelings or experiences of teens.

Timely entrance into the triune doors and leading in the triune dance

To understand the importance of a balanced view of the Trinity two further images may help. One is to see the Trinity as like a three sectioned (but without glass divisions!) revolving door whose entry point or point of emphasis will differ depending on one's time and circumstance. However, very soon in the development of a youth ministry we need to be moving through and relating to all three: Father, Son and Spirit; Creator, Reconciler and Redeemer/Consummator. The Father and Spirit cannot be understood clearly without Christ.

The second image picks up on the idea of Trinitarian indwelling or *perichoresis* as derived from the word for a dance. In the Trinitarian dance towards the kingdom, at certain stages of the divine economy or work one member will take the lead, the Father in creation, the Son in reconciliation and the Spirit in redemption/consummation.[31] But often in our theologies and youth work one member hogs the lead, treading on the toes of the others! We may be overly focused on the Father's (primarily) creative work, or the Son's reconciling work, or the Spirit's gifting, redeeming work.

---

31. All three are involved in each other's work too, but in the doctrine of the Trinitarian appropriations one has the leading role in that task or job - it is his primary calling.

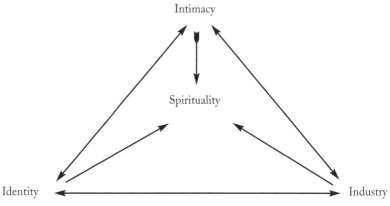

Two dimensional representation of the RLT Model.

Vocation as a way out of the vicious circle of self

The prescription I propose for our hyper/postmodern problems of social and identity erosion under the deluge of individualism is a return to the biblical and Reformed notion of vocation tying public and private, role and real self together. This is linked to the Trinity as a 'compressed narrative'[32] or story in which we find our character or identity. Only then will the empty modern self be filled and we will be free to be who we are called to be.

A creation basis for self as vocation (McFadyen)

A broader and more dynamic creation and anthropological basis for a theology of self as vocation relates the person to their purpose or calling(s) in a 'dialogical' conception of human personhood as a middle way between individualism and communitarianism.[33]

In creation, the primal calling to be of creation and humanity, the 'let us make' precedes the 'be fruitful'. This is both gift and task, an indicative which is an implicit imperative to be what you are called into being to be. It is a 'being in gratitude'.[34] The individuality established in

---

32. J. Fowler, 'Adolescence in the Trinitarian Praxis of God', in J. Fowler et al., *Christ and the Adolescent: A Theological Approach to Youth Ministry* (Princeton Theological Seminary, 1996), 13–22.
33. Alistair McFadyen, *The Call to Personhood: A Christian Theory of the Individual in Social Relationships* (Cambridge: Cambridge University Press, 1990), 9, drawing on Barth, Moltmann and communications theory.
34. McFadyen, 20–21.

dialogue with God's word is fractured with the Fall, but re-created through God's calling and re-naming (giving new identity) of Abram as Abraham (Genesis 17:5), Simon as Peter (John 1:40–42) and Saul as Paul (Acts 13:9). Christ's call to the disciples to become 'fishers of men' (Mark 1:16–20) enables them to stand out as individuals from their context, re-creating them in a new corporate context.[35] Our calling in Scripture, whether to prophethood, discipleship or apostleship, constitute our identity. We are what we are called.

This pattern of sedimented communication, or layer upon layer of calling, through which we are called forth by our relations with significant others, especially God, is 'an ontological structure, something like an "order of creation".'[36] Through the process of promise giving and promise keeping (as one book title, *Man the Promising Primate* suggests) and

> the expectations others have of us ... through their form of address ... the identity of a person is formed or deformed through the calls of others and God .... The distorted call is an attempt to establish both a distorted relation and a distorted self-presence which one wants the other to believe to be a genuine identity. An undistorted address, on the other hand, recognises the recipient as an independent subject of communication who is not overdetermined by the call. This recognition creates space within the relation for the other's independent communication. It is only through the undistorted call of others that the call of Christ and the conditions of existence in the divine image are socially refracted and mediated in interpersonal relations.[37]

Our churches and youth groups are meant to be re-calling people in this way. To illustrate, if a young person has only ever been called clumsy, ugly, stupid, from day one, those distorted calls, particularly from significant others or those who should be in intimate relationships with the person, will distort his/her sense of identity. If, however, the person is called by name as God's beloved child, as beautiful, full of potential, gifted, for all his/her faults and sin, he/she will have a healthy

---

35. McFadyen, 46–48.
36. McFadyen, 71.
37. McFadyen, 116–120. Compare educational research on the effect of teacher expectations, and the movie *Stand and Deliver* based on a true story of a teacher of a group of black students who had been labelled no hopers. Through re-calling them affirmatively the teacher enabled them to win a group maths prize. Contrast the effect of destructive 'calling' in the SBS documentary on 6 May 1998 'About Us: A Class Divided', when teacher Jane Elliott divided her class on the basis of blue or brown eyes, favouring and affirming the brown-eyed kids, while the blue-eyed soon internalised their 'called' inferiority.

sense of self before God. But increasingly, through abuse, family, educational and work 'failure', a prolonged sense of dependence, through manipulative advertising leading to distorted body image, many younger people come to us with a seriously damaged sense of self that needs to be 're-called', almost like a car manufacturer recalls a damaged car.

This will not happen individualistically though, in some 70s *Ice Storm* search for individual identity, peeling back layer upon layer of the onion, or as in the musical *Mass,* where the priest strips back layer after layer of liturgical robes till he stands near naked saying 'there's just me', as if the real self can be separated completely from its roles and responsibilities. The self can only be discovered relationally, communally, over time, and in the 'death' that is discipleship (Mark 8:35–36). We are only 'naked selves' ultimately before God, as Calvin shows,[38] and in the context of mutual vulnerability in an accepting Christian community.

Eschatological and Spirit based mobile vocations in a mobile world (Moltmann)

From an eschatological or Spirit-centred perspective Moltmann agrees with McFadyen. The point of reference, identity and integration amid our complex variety of roles is not in some modern 'transcendental Ego' or real self, self-consciously rising like an Everest above the plains of our daily roles, but in the call to 'the mission of Christian hope'. Social callings or roles are then judged not in terms of self-realisation (the focus of too much youth work), but in terms of incarnating or concretely anticipating the coming kingdom. This is the criterion for choice and changing of callings. It also warns us against putting all our eggs in any earthly vocational basket such as employment, especially as there are so few jobs for younger people.[39]

Further, for Moltmann, with a touch of postmodern exaggeration, humanity has no nature, only a history. 'Man and his conditions become more mobile, changeable and movable than they ever were before'. The vocational corollary is the statement that 'Vocation for life

---

38. See Mouw, *God Who Commands,* Chapter 4.
39. Jürgen Moltmann, *Theology of Hope: On the Ground and the Implications of a Christian Eschatology,* trans. James W. Leitch (San Francisco: Harper Collins, 1991 [1967]), 329–334.

is replaced by a job for a particular space of time'.[40] Moltmann thus brings a sense of eschatological (end-time) elasticity to the secularising and domestication of vocation into a life-long career.

Yet the danger in some (charismatic and Pentecostal) Spirit-based approaches to youth work, for all their strengths, is that the experience of the eschatological and supernatural spiritual gifts, especially tongues and healing, is often stressed as an identity marker of the young Christian. Further, because the Spirit is confined to the church and is not seen as the Creator Spirit (Genesis 1:2, Psalm 104:30, Romans 8:20–27), creative and natural talents and normal work as avenues of service and vocation get ignored.

Christocentric calling

Similarly, radically Christocentric and exclusively evangelistic approaches stress that calling is only calling to conversion and the kingdom, and that Jesus called his disciples away from their jobs to follow him (as Barth and more so St Matthias Centennial Park and most AFES youth work stresses). However, this is also often to the neglect of peoples' studies and work as vocations or dimensions of service in God's creation. Jesus also regularly called those he healed, like the Gadarene demoniac in Mark 5, to take their healing back home with them, to stay where they were called, just as Paul said 'remain in the condition [that is, sphere of service] in which you were called' (that is, converted, 1 Corinthians 7:20; compare 17, 24, 29–31). Both dimensions of Christian vocation are important: both the Adamic, creational, called to stay, continuity dimension; and the Abrahamic, Exodus, christological, eschatological, mobile, called away, flexibility dimension – within an over-arching three articled Trinitarian approach.

The self as a relational network – identity, intimacy, industry

The need for a Trinitarian and balanced relationship of identity and vocation is backed up from psychological sources. An American pastoral counsellor, Peter Schreck, has found that the dominant therapeutic individualist model was inadequate and unbiblical. The key questions people came to him with were: (a) Who am I? – about gaining self; (b) With whom am I close? – sharing self; (c) What am I

---

40. Moltmann, *Planning*, 109.

to do with my life – investing self; and (d) How will I be whole (or saved) – saving self. In turn he 'equated these four questions with the concerns of identity, intimacy, industry and integrity (spirituality) respectively.' None of these 'relational life tasks' can be accomplished individually, for they are all interpersonal. They also fit our Trinitarian model well, being 'anchored in the theological concepts of creation, incarnation, redemption and the Kingdom of God'. This provides a good framework for youth work (see diagram on page 147). Schreck designed an exercise where each person imagines they have twelve chips representing personal resources (time, energy, money, talents and so on) and then distributes them among the four relational life tasks according to how the person normally distributes them. It is a helpful exercise for determining how balanced our youth work is.[41]

Conclusion

I began by setting the context for youth work in the postmodern sense of de-centred, fragmenting or saturated selves. To this I added the lack of public time and space available for younger people in an increasingly privatised world. I then contrasted this to the Trinitarian God who makes time and space for us and allows us to enter into his own trialogue, giving us voice. This dialogical model and a balanced stress on each member of the Trinity's distinctive vocations, and calling of the individual in a distinctive, but communal way, provides a dynamic but stable and integrated sense of identity, intimacy and industry, not a postmodern disintegration of the self. It provides a biblical and viable model for youth work in a postmodern context.

---

41. G. Peter Schreck, Professor of Pastoral Care and Counselling at Eastern Baptist Theological Seminary, Philadelphia, PA. 'Personhood and Relational Life Tasks: A Model for Integrating Psychology and Theology', unpublished paper. There is a similarity to developmental theorists like Erik Erikson, *Childhood and Society*, (New York: Norton, 1950) and *Identity and the Life Cycle* (New York: Norton, 1980), D. Levinson, *The Seasons of a Man's Life* (New York: Alfred A. Knopf, 1978) and J. Fowler, *Stages of Faith: The Psychology of Human Development and the Quest for Meaning* (San Francisco: Harper & Row, 1981), but without their strict sense of sequence.

CHAPTER ELEVEN

Discipline, a reflective conversation
Roger Bray

'Those who think that the Church can stand for long without the bond of discipline are mistaken.'[1]

The situation

It had been a long Friday night. I found Ben, one of my new youth leaders, about to wash out someone's mouth with soap for swearing. I quickly intervened, but the leader protested loudly. He declared his actions would be an appropriate punishment for someone who had broken one of the commandments by using our Lord's name in vain. The young leader went on to explain that this was what his mother had done with him, and it was a reasonable form of discipline.[2]

Later on in my office with three youth ministry students, I took the opportunity to use this situation as a catalyst for us as leaders to talk about the issue of discipline. With the proviso that we not gossip about the person involved, we discussed the particulars of the situation, with a major emphasis on an exploration of ideas and understanding.

I began by asking how, in general, discipline problems should be handled.

An approach to discipline

George (second year Bachelor of Theology Youth Ministry) had just done an essay on this topic and the method of discipline he had thought about included the following principles.

---

1. John Calvin, *Institutes of the Christian Religion,* ed. J.T. McNeill; tr. F.L. Battles, LCC XX & XXI (Philadelphia: Fortress, 1960), IV xii 4.
2. Situation based on real event.

Plan to limit discipline problems by:

1. clearly defining expectations and consequences of misbehaviour for the group regularly;
2. considering the effect of the environment you create; and
3. considering your own example.

When correcting behaviour:

1. ask is it necessary to correct the behaviour?
2. be firm and outline why the behaviour is unacceptable and what may be the consequences, but don't argue;
3. don't embarrass the person in front of others;
4. be a good listener; and
5. ensure that in the process no one else comes to harm.

In light of recent developments:

1. don't use physical force;
2. don't be alone in a room with only one child;
3. don't expose people to danger to teach them a lesson; and
4. inform parents and the main leader where necessary.[3]

I proposed that we find out what the Bible has to say about discipline by doing a quick survey of some of the relevant texts.

Old Testament survey

In the Old Testament, the word most often translated discipline is *yasar* which means to hasten or instruct. The two derivatives are *yissor* and *musar*.[4]

The first use of the word is in Leviticus 26 where the writer is coming to the end of a section known as the Holiness code in which God's people are exhorted to be holy. Chapter 26 outlines a list of

---

3. Based on N. Halliday, 'Dealing with Discipline', *Camping Magazine* (July-August 1993), 16–20 and S. Heslehurst, 'Discipline', *Child Protection Policy and Reporting Procedures* (Sydney: Unpublished, 1998).
4. P. Gilchrist, *The Theological Word Book of the Old Testament* (Chicago: Moody, 1980), 386–387.

accompanying blessings and curses. In verses 18 and 28 God's *yasar* is evident in the punishment God exacts as a result of the covenant being broken. Verse 23 makes it clear, however, that the purpose of the punishment is to restore God's people to himself.[5]

In Deuteronomy, the book of covenant renewal, God is seen as a Father in relation to how he has acted in salvation history (Deuteronomy 1:31).[6] In Moses' second speech, this understanding is associated with discipline: 'Know then in your heart that as a parent disciplines a child so the Lord your God disciplines you' (8:5). This statement comes in the context of God stating that he led the people of Israel into the wilderness in order to test their hearts (8:2). Indeed 'this discipline then might be considered education that is theocentric, indeed, theofugal'.[7] The image of father and child suggests a loving filial relationship.

Let's take a look at some wisdom literature. In Proverbs 1:7, discipline is associated with wisdom, the fear of Yahweh and instruction. Gilchrist concludes that 'Proverbs and other wisdom literature speak of discipline with the emphasis on instruction' in God's ways.[8]

In addition, in Proverbs 3:11–12 we find out that the *musar* of Yahweh is for those whom the Lord loves. Gilchrist makes the point that 'discipline gives assurance of sonship'.[9]

More generally in the prophets, the theme of *musar* is developed in that God 'reveals His discipline through his mighty acts in history to the people of Israel and Judah in particular and to the nations in general'.[10] God deals with his people in the Old Testament from the standpoint of a loving Father.

Therefore, in the Old Testament God's fatherly discipline is closely connected with his unfolding purposes for his people. God's discipline is an activity of salvation history, and indeed as God disciplines he reveals his salvation plan. In addition, discipline's primary tools are warnings and corrections in the context of instruction. Punitive measures are used as a last resort, and their purpose is to restore people into covenant relationship with God.

---

5. Gilchrist, 386–387.
6. W. Dumbrell, *The Faith of Israel* (Leicester: Apollos, 1993), 53.
7. Gilchrist, 386–387.
8. Gilchrist, 386–387.
9. Gilchrist, 386–387.
10. Gilchrist, 386–387.

Ultimately however disobedience to the Law and resistance to God's discipline has meant that in God's redemptive plan Jesus bears the punishment that we deserve and establishes a new covenant. This event is foreshadowed in Isaiah 53:5. Here, where the Suffering Servant is in full focus, we read these words, 'But he was wounded for our transgressions, crushed for our iniquities; upon him was the *yasar* that made us whole, and by his bruises we are healed'.

God's ultimate discipline has fallen on Christ, and, yet again, it is in order that we might be restored into a covenant relationship with Him.

Reflection on the situation

Chris, another student, interjected at this point: 'Hang on – what you're saying is that the measures that Ben took tonight have no Old Testament support, let alone, I imagine, New Testament support.'

Julie, the third student added, 'But Ben comes from a solid Christian family. Why would he act this way?'

In my assessment there are a number of issues which intersect at this point regarding discipline.

From my experience the majority of youth leaders and indeed youth ministers are fairly pragmatic when it comes to issues of discipline. They do what works for them. For a number this includes doing what their parents did or what they saw done at school.

In Ben's case, his parents reacted strongly to the significant change that took place in discipline policy in schools in the 1970s. They belonged to a school of thought which said that 'In order to form the minds of children, the first thing to be done was to conquer their will and bring them to obedient temper'. The intended result was that the child would be 'capable of being governed by the reason and piety of its parents, till their own understanding comes to maturity, and the principles of religion have taken root in the mind'.[11]

In contrast, educational policy in schools from the 1970s onward suggested a far less authoritarian approach. The policy was that 'Students are persons and should enjoy the normal rights of the

---

11. From a letter to John Wesley, dated July 24, 1732, quoted by R.L. Harmon, *Susanna, Mother of the Wesleys* (London: Hodder & Stoughton, 1968), 59.

individual', indeed that students should have a written body of rights.[12]

Julie commented: 'So you could say that Ben's parents' reaction to the changes in discipline is typical of the fundamentalist approach.'

When I asked her what she meant, she quoted from Packer:

> Fundamentalism is now a religious attitude rather than a religious movement. It is a highly ideological attitude. It is intransigent and inflexible; it expects conformity; it fears academic liberty. It makes no allowance for the inconsistent, and thus partially valid, elements in other positions.[13]

Certainly with respect to discipline it would appear that some Christian parents have a highly ideological attitude, which is combined with their theology and practice. It is a particularly difficult issue to deal with because parents who think like this find it difficult to listen to alternate views. What is of more concern is that some of our employers still think like this.

On the other hand many parents and employers have reconsidered their ideas and have made significant adjustments.

George posed the question, 'So what makes this older and sometimes fundamentalist view attractive for Christians?'

Behind the scenes

Gunton, in his book *The Promise of Trinitarian Theology*, argues that Augustine had a tendency to develop an understanding of man in Neoplatonic categories.[14] This meant that the human links to God must be non-corporal.

For example, Augustine in discussing the trinity and love argues:

---

12. 'Annual Conference 1973', *Education,* Journal of New South Wales Teachers' Federation (Jan 30 1974), 10.
13. J. Packer, *The Word of God and Fundamentalism* (London: Church Book Room Press, 1961), 105. In addition note The Fundamentalism Project, a study conducted by the American Academy of Arts and Sciences, has observed: 'Fundamentalism has appeared as a tendency, a habit of mind, found within religious communities and paradigmatically embodied in certain representative individuals and movements, which manifests itself as a strategy, or set of strategies, by which beleaguered believers attempt to preserve their distinctive identity as a people or group. Feeling this identity at risk in the contemporary era, they fortify it by a selective retrieval of doctrines, beliefs and practices from a sacred past.' M. Marty and R. Appleby (eds), *Fundamentalisms Observed* (Chicago: University of Chicago Press, 1991), 835.
14. C. Gunton, *The Promise of Trinitarian Theology* (Edinburgh: T&T Clark, 1991), 106.

> It is not the fact that mind and spirit belong to a particular human being that determines that they are minds and spirit. Remove whatever it is that, being added, constitutes a human being (that is the body), and mind and spirit will still remain.[15]

The result is that in regard to the doctrine of humankind, it has traditionally been asserted that humans are a functional whole but comprised of two parts: a soul and a body. In this schema the mind has been associated with the non-corporal world.

The problem is that in the 17th century Descartes, in developing rationalism, builds on this understanding, and takes the ontological dimension further suggesting that the human condition can be summed up by the axiom; *Cogito ergo sum* (I think, therefore I am). One of the implications of this emphasis on the mind and reason has been that there has been an 'exaltation of the formal rule of thought to the status of divine law in relation to which all else is criticised'.[16]

In regard, then, to ontology of humans these particular ideas have had a significant influence on theories of ethical behaviour. These influences include a stress on duty and obligation to certain reasoned principles or divine laws. In addition, there has been an emphasis on consequences with a focus on the individual and his/her inner dimensions.[17]

This emphasis is still with us. The change in focus in the 1970s regarding discipline, while helpful in changing the perception of who children are, is still very individualistic. These ideas and the resulting consequentialist perception of discipline is alive and well. In addition, there is an increased emphasis on an individual's rights and choice.

Julie asked me, 'But you don't disagree with all of that do you?'

My response is 'not completely', but I do want to suggest a different perspective – one that is more consistent with a biblical theological view.

---

15. A. McGrath, *The Christian Theology Reader* (Massachusetts: Blackwell, 1995), 101.
16. O. O'Donovan, *Resurrection and Moral Order: An Outline of Evangelical Ethics* (Grand Rapids: Eerdmans, 1994), 134. M. Polanyi in *Personal Knowledge: Towards a post critical philosophy* (London: Routledge, 1962) Chapter 1 observes, that the Copernican revolution, popularly conceived as having displaced man from the centre of the universe by establishing heliocentrism, in fact rather did the opposite. In place of his senses man found the power of the mind to conceptualise systems with universal application.
17. Note for Kant punishment should be purely retributive. He suggests that punishment should only result because we have, under the moral law, a duty to do so.

A fundamental shift required in framework

The death of Jesus is a significant turning point in God's salvation plan. What does this mean for us and discipline?

In *Resurrection and Moral Order: An Outline of Evangelical Ethics* Oliver O'Donovan argues that

> by virtue of the fact that there is a creator, there is also a creation that is ordered to the creator. But then just because it's ordered vertically in this way, it must also have an internal horizontal ordering amongst its path. Out of these two fundamental directions of created order, we form the concepts of order as end and kind as teleological and generic order.[18]

By implication when there is disorder in these orders there is sin. But with the resurrection of Jesus we have the reversal of 'Adam's choice of sin and death', and the reversal of this order.[19]

Important to understanding this significant reversal is that we have in Christ God's intended *telos* for us and the resulting teleological order.

To explore this a Trinitarian perspective is helpful. In regard to teleological order J.B. Torrance in *Worship Community and the Triune God of Grace*,[20] establishes for us, by using a Trinitarian view of the gospel, that there is a twofold relation of communion, mutual indwelling and perichoretic union:

a) between Jesus and the Father and the Spirit into which we are drawn to participate

b) between Christ and his body in communion in the Spirit and between the members of the body life in the spirit.[21]

This suggests that the human person is one who finds his or her true being *(telos)* in relation in love and in communion.

In other words as regards our *telos* 'We have been created by God to find our true being in communion, in sonship, in mutual personal relationships of love'.[22] Torrance goes on to suggest that 'God created us, male and female, in his image to find our true humanity in

---

18. O'Donovan, 32.
19. O'Donovan, 13.
20. J.B. Torrance, *Worship Community and the Triune God of Grace* (Carlisle: Paternoster Press, 1996).
21. Torrance, 20–21.
22. Torrance, 26–27.

perichoretic unity with him and one another, and who renews us in his image in Christ. Jesus said, as the father has loved me, so I have loved you, so ought you to love one another (John 15:9–13)'.[23]

Therefore our true nature is found in communion with God in relation to others. It is not found through obeying a series of laws to be obedient to God. Rather, it is about the context of relationships lived out in obedience to Jesus as a result in his love for us. Discipline then fits within a mutual love framework, and by implication its *telos* is mutual love in the context of a Christian community. Discipline is not therefore primarily about ensuring that others dutifully maintain a set of obligations or set standards, or primarily about consequences or choices of the individual.

New Testament survey

With O'Donovan's and Torrance's frameworks in mind, let's turn to what the New Testament has to say.

In the Old Testament, discipline is in the context of God's fatherly unfolding of his purposes in working with his people. God's primary tool has been instruction, with punitive measures as a last resort. Its purpose was to restore people into the covenant relationship with God to God's order.

In the Greek New Testament the Hebrew equivalent of *yasar* is *'paideia'* and its cogent verbal form which is *'paideuo'*. The root of the word is *'pais'* which is 'a child'.[24] This suggests that the term has significant filial associations.

In addition, Alan Langdon in his thesis *Parental Responsibility in Education* maintains that linguistically these words involve the concept of caring and guiding, instructing and teaching, correcting and chastening.[25] These concepts are particularly evident in Hebrews 12:2–11. Hebrews, using the genre of a homily, urges believers to persevere in their pilgrimage. With reference to the Old Testament, Hebrews develops an eschatological focus based on the fulfilment brought by the work of Christ 'the pioneer and perfecter of our faith' (Hebrews 12:2).

---

23. Torrance, 26–27.
24. A. Langdon, *Parental Responsibility in Education* (Sydney: Unpublished Masters Thesis, Sydney University, 1976), 57.
25. Langdon, 57.

The passage urges believers to persevere and to endure hardship as discipline. The discussion that follows makes clear that while a human father's discipline may be helpful, it is flawed (verse 10). God's discipline on the other hand is for his own people and is characterised by caring, correcting and education. The telos is righteousness and peace, which is consistent with the restoration of God's order and a mutual love *telos*.

George interjected at this point: 'Hardship is linked to discipline? That sounds strange.'

I agreed with him, but it makes more sense when you look back at Hebrews 5:8 and see the example of Jesus. Here a link is made between Jesus' suffering and his learning of obedience and his perfection. From these passages, it would appear that suffering/hardship is linked to teaching us to respond in obedience in order that we might be perfected. This link between hardship and discipline is consistent with what happened in the Old Testament. The effect of this view is that our perspective on hardship changes when we see it as part of God's discipline. The result of this discipline is our being perfected, or movement towards our *telos*.

With this is in mind, let's examine Paul's disciplinary practice. References include Romans 16:17; 1 Corinthians 5:1–13, 16:22; 2 Corinthians 13:1–2; Galatians 6:1–5; 2 Thessalonians 3:6–15; 1 Timothy 1:8–20, 5:19–22 and Titus 3:10–11.[26]

Consistent with the teaching of Jesus in Matthew 7:1–5 and 18:21–35, Paul's disciplinary practice (Galatians 6:1-5) suggests that the first step regarding the erring believer, was to be personal, private and gentle. More generally in regard to the actions of the discipliner, Schmidt notes, 'the stress of the discipline passages is on humility, readiness to forgive on the part of the person who admonishes. Indeed it is evident from these passages, that Paul's disciplinary practices were intended to be remedial rather than punitive messages'.[27] This clearly supports the Old Testament position that we have examined.

What happens if an individual doesn't respond to the warnings? In 1 Corinthians 5 there has been an incident of incest. The church is

---

26. T. Schmidt, 'Discipline' in F.G. Hawthorne and P.M. Martin (eds), *Dictionary of Paul and his Letters* (Leicester: IVP, 1993), 215.
27. Schmidt, 215.

arrogant and boastful and has had a fairly relaxed attitude towards the situation.

In verses 1–2 Paul states that he knows about the problem and suggests that the man be put outside the believing community (verses 2, 4–5, 7 and 13). He then outlines why they are to carry out the expulsion, and finally in verses 9–13 returns to the church's attitude.[28]

What is important here is that in verse 5, the handing over of the man to Satan is in order that his spirit may be saved on the day of the Lord. In other words, it is consistent with the view that we have already stated: that discipline in Paul's case is not so much punitive, but rather to restore the person to the believing community.

Schmidt sums up his article on discipline by suggesting a look at Philippians 2:1–5.[29] Although, as Schmidt notes, it does not address discipline directly, it does express precisely the principle behind the references to the subject

> It is the incentive of love, the sharing of the spirit, the humble attitude, that is, the mind of Christ that makes it possible to hold another person accountable. Thus, the secret power of effective discipline is its reflective element. That is, the one who holds another accountable, is first accountable to be a loving person. When this is true of a community of believers, isolation of the offender will be a compelling remedial force. Ultimately then, it is not the power of persuasion or coercion that affects recall, but the power of love emanating from a transformed community.[30]

From this very brief survey what becomes evident is that the Old Testament principles have been reapplied in the context of the New Covenant community.

Discipline: self control

The New Testament also introduces another concept. Discipline is associated with self-control. The main word is *enkrateia*, power-control over one's self or over some thing.[31]

Again the influence of Augustine and the dual ontological nature of

---

28. G.D. Fee, *The First Epistle to the Corinthians* NICOT (Grand Rapids: Eerdmans, 1987), 197.
29. Schmidt, 218.
30. Schmidt, 218.
31. M. Hill, 'Paul's Concept of *Enkrateia*', *RTR* Vol xxxvi (Sept-Dec 1977), 70.

human kind is evident in these discussions. In this scenario, reason functions as the prime means by which we are self-controlled. This has the effect of sending us in the direction of the Stoics, which involves a kind of self-discipline or power over oneself.[32]

In contrast to this we are called to live life in the spirit, 'participating through the Spirit in the incarnate Son's communion with the Father'.[33] Galatians 5:1–26 reminds us that we are to live life by the Spirit (verse 16) so that we are free to obey the law. The law is summed up in a singe command 'love your neighbour as yourself' (verse 14). This is consistent with our *telos*.

It is in this context that Paul then goes on to list the fruits of the Spirit (verses 22–26). Within these fruits is *enkrateia*. Baltensweiler concludes, and I agree, that 'the possibility of fashioning one's life in the way God desires is never something firmly at one's disposal. It must always be received afresh as the gift of the Spirit'.[34]

The implication of these insights is that self-discipline is about the 'regulation of the whole of life and its re-orientation towards goals which are God given'.[35] It comes about because of the work of the Spirit in our lives, not through self-mastery or the mastery of others.

George summed up our theological discussion: 'What you're saying really challenges much of what we're doing in discipline in terms of behaviour management and the current understanding of discipline and the consequential approach.'

The application

Julie began trying to apply the theology to our situation: 'Clearly Ben needs to be disciplined. You might approach Ben and talk with him about his view of discipline. Basically he needs to get a hold of himself and calm down.'

I commented, 'That sounds a bit like self mastery doesn't it?'

'I suppose so,' said Julie.

---

32. Hill, 77.
33. Torrance, 20.
34. H. Baltensweiler, 'Enkrateia', *The New International Dictionary of New Testament Theology* Vol 1 (Grand Rapids: Paternoster, 1986), 497.
35. Hill, 78.

George added: 'Perhaps you might also encourage him to try and restore his relationship with the youth group member and to apologise?'

I believe that is important, but I would also identify what areas Ben needs to grow in if he is going to live by the Spirit as Christ intended. What I mean is that while the overarching *telos* of the human is mutual love relationships, there are certain characteristics, certain virtues that you would expect of followers of Christ. Not 'virtues which enable an individual to discharge a certain role or even achieve a certain success' but rather virtues which are the expression of a person moving towards a certain *telos*.[36]

To achieve this I would want to spend some time building a better relationship with Ben and help him see what it means to be in Christ and motivated by the love of Christ. Clearly that would also help in dealing with some of those inter-personal issues and his understanding of the role of the Ten Commandments.

George raised the question: 'But what do we do with the boy who swore?'

Once again I would want to ask the same questions about characteristics of followers of Christ, and proceed from there. I imagine the boy may be very confused and it may take some sorting out. But my hope is that he can forgive Ben.

George also pointed out that I would probably need to approach the boy's parents about what Ben did and explain the situation.

I'll finish with two other reflections. There is a new push by schools to involve parents in formulating discipline issues. My question is: How do we respond to this? Also, what is our role in helping parents of our young people respond to discipline issues?

Secondly, take time to reflect on your own discipline policies. I think they will reflect what your intended *telos* is for the group.

I hope I've raised some issues for you to think about.

---

36. A. MacIntyre, *After Virtue: A study of moral theory* (Indiana: University of Notre Dame Press, 1984), 185.

CHAPTER TWELVE

The charismatic leader, change and the institutionalised church

David Rietveld

My own church/youth group experience

When I was younger I attended a church of about 150 members. It was a fairly comfortable little set-up, at least for those who attended. Everyone who came, came every week and sat in exactly the same seat. In fact sometimes for fun, my brother and I would go and move people's hymnbooks during the week. It amused us to see the confusion and frustration this caused.

We had just enough people to pay the minister and all our other expenses. While it would have been great if more people came it was important to us that nobody left. So we tended to do things the same way we always had so as not to upset the current members. We didn't really impact our local community greatly, though a few local young people came to our children's programs. When they hit teenage years they stopped coming.

We had a youth group. It was made up entirely of children from church families. We always struggled to gain a 'critical mass'; to have enough people so that it didn't feel awkward. There were of course a few youth in the church who didn't come because they were too cool. But then they only ever went to church to keep their parents happy, and over time they came less and less.

On the whole, services were boring. As a concession to this feeling among the youth, we were allowed to sing a few songs with a guitar before the service began. Yet it always felt as if this was a token gesture, and nothing else ever changed. It felt as if the older people were making allowances for us, rather than seeking to include us. Getting more involved in the ministry of the church meant coming on board with the existing directions of the church, and joining one of the various committees. There was no forum to discuss why we did any of the things we did, only avenues to become involved in their maintenance. From what I can gather, the church hasn't changed much. No, that's not true. They built a new car park which was nearer the front door as the aging congregation couldn't walk as far.

Perhaps you can relate to some of my experiences. In fact come to think of it, many of the churches I have attended have been not unlike the one I have just described. Why is it that stagnation resulting in a slow death so often characterises our churches? This is particularly odd when it seems from the biblical account that both personal spiritual and numerical growth is to be expected in the life of the Christian community.[1]

While according to the National Church Life Survey 1996 (NCLS96) Australian churches grew on average by 6% over the previous 5 years,[2] yet Hughes et al paint a gloomy picture of the preceding era as one of 'substantial decline [in] the mainline Protestant and Anglican Churches'.[3] Even if one can find a church that at one time has a spurt of substantial growth, chances are that at some point the growth slows or ceases – as if there were some kind of ceiling preventing further growth.

Thus we turn to our main question, namely 'Why do churches stop growing?' Evangelicals tell us that it is because we no longer proclaim the truths of the gospel.[4] Pentecostals tell us it is because we have quenched the power of the Spirit.[5] Leadership experts tell us that it is because our leaders lack vision.[6] Still others will suggest that the physical constraints of the building will inhibit growth.[7] In fact there appear to be as many answers as there are areas of expertise.

---

1. 'I am the vine, you are the branches. Those who abide in me and I in them bear much fruit' (John 15:5).
2. P. Kaldor et al, *NCLS 96*.
3. P. Hughes et al, *Believe it or not: Australian Spirituality and the Churches in the 90s* (Melbourne: New Litho Pty Ltd, 1995), 10.
4. J.W. Woodhouse, 'Evangelism and Social Responsibility', *Christians in Society* (ed B.G. Webb; Sydney: Lancer, 1988), 20–23.
5. J. Deere, *Surprised by the Power of the Holy Spirit* (Grand Rapids: Zondervan, 1993), 222–227.
6. J.C. Maxwell, *Developing the Leader Within You* (Nashville: Thomas Nelson, 1993).
7. R.H. Schuller, *Your Church Has Real Possibilities* (Glendale, California: Regal Books, 1974), 19–22.

An overview of Max Weber

Max Weber, one of the founding fathers of sociology, offers an explanation for the cessation of growth. His particular interest is in the questions of power and change. How is it that the current structures are legitimised? On what authority do the leaders within structures act? And how can the current order be changed? Briefly speaking, a Weberian account of church growth will highlight the 'institutionalisation' of the dynamic processes of the church. Thomas O'Dea, developing Weber's thesis, argues that in time the institutionalised church will become increasingly irrelevant to those outside its structures. This will be most clearly seen at the intake points for the church – among the youth – and this in turn inhibits new growth.

For Weber the impetus for change will lie in the 'charismatic' leader; whom people will naturally follow. His role will be to challenge the existing norms and structures, and to re-introduce dynamism into the processes. The result is that the church will again become relevant to outsiders (and youth), and a new period of growth will ensue.

However, there is a history of charismatic leaders using their charisma to encourage people to follow them, rather than challenging the existing norms. Charismatic leaders, or 'prophets' as Weber calls them, are necessarily defined in opposition to the system. There is therefore an inherent tension in their ability integrate their 'disciples' into that system, or into the new system that their movement eventually becomes.

Trinitarian theology, however, demands that all members of the church, be they old and traditional or young and dynamic, be part of the one body just as the Godhead is one (John 17:21). Any progressive Christian youth leader will need to maintain the tension between on the one hand belonging personally to the existing community and bringing youth into it, and on the other hand seeking to change that system so that it becomes more relevant to those outside that system whom the leader is trying to reach.

Sociology and religion

Before we take a closer look at Max Weber's theory, we need to undertake a brief analysis of the relationship between sociology and religion. Sociology as such is not concerned with a search for truth.

Rather it is concerned with social facts.[8] In this case it seeks to give an account of the origins of religion that explains its relationship to society and the economic order.[9]

Sociology's explanations are not necessarily at odds with theological explanations of social facts. Rather it offers a subset of insights into reality; shaped by the questions that it asks and the presuppositions it makes. Given that theological explanations are established in absolute truth, namely the revealed Word of God, its insights are foundational and unable to be contradicted. Sociological insights are, on the other hand, contingent.

Yet this does not preclude sociology from offering a unique set of insights into religion and its social forms. As a descriptive discipline, sociology's insights will be in the realm of describing the way things are, and the processes underlying that reality that maintain the *status quo*. Armed with these insights we will be better equipped to think about how to tackle and change the dysfunctional systems that so often paralyse our churches.[10]

Weber: The prophet and the process of routinisation

For Weber, new religious movements are most likely to begin with a 'prophet'. A prophet is 'a purely individual bearer of charisma, who by virtue of his mission proclaims a religious doctrine or divine commandment'.[11] The prophet provides both the initial burst of energy and grounding cluster of ideas which will either establish a completely new religion, or radically alter an existing one.

Because of their radical nature, prophets will rarely emanate from an existing priesthood. Rather they will tend to come from among the laity, and define themselves against the existing structures. They will reject the past, and are in this sense revolutionary.[12] Prophets will offer a

---

8. Granted there is here an inherent assumption in sociology that the way things are is the way they ought to be. Thus social facts are not totally value-free as often claimed.
9. M. Hewitt, 'Sociology of Religion', *A New Dictionary of Sociology* (ed G. Duncan Mitchell; London: RKP, 1985), 214.
10. D.A. Fraser and A. Campolo, *Sociology Through the Eyes of Faith* (San Francisco: Harper, 1992), 27-60, 291-307. Note that Campolo lacks an appreciation of the theology found in special revelation.
11. M. Weber, *Economy and Society* (New York: 1968) vol 2, 426.
12. M. Weber, *Prophets and the Routinisation of Charisma* (ed. R. Gill; London: Geoffrey Chapman, 1987), 161.

new coherent worldview doctrine that is at the same time practical. It will encourage a 'consciously integrated and meaningful attitude toward life'.[13]

In order to establish a new movement, prophets need to gather followers around themselves. Note these followers are 'personal devotees' who often support the prophet financially in return for following his/her route to salvation. Contrast this with the institutionalised church, where a hierarchy of 'elders, deacons, and lay' support the **office** of 'priesthood', rather than the current incumbent.[14]

The prophet's haphazard gathering of followers will in turn become an organised congregation. If for no other reason than financial, the personal devotees will organise themselves into a permanent organisation with rights and responsibilities. The ideas of the prophet will be codified into a coherent set of doctrines, and the followers will become either exponents of or adherents to that teaching.[15]

A priesthood emerges, whose task it is to codify the doctrines, and to continue to teach and reinforce the standards as demanded by the set of formalised doctrine (which is in the process of becoming a sacred text). Yet while this priest has both status and power, he/she is dependent upon the laity for a livelihood. The priest must therefore regularly service their needs so as to maintain his/her own standing and authority.[16]

For the purposes of this paper we will not specifically explore an account of the origin of Christian religion. However it is worth mentioning that an overview of Weber's account enables one to appreciate the value of this framework in explaining the ministry of Jesus (as the prophet); his relationship to his disciples and to the Levitical priesthood; and the function of Paul (as the codifying priest who established institutionalised churches).[17]

---

13. Weber, *Economy and Society*, 451, A. Giddens, *Capitalism and Modern Social Theory: An analysis of the writings of Marx, Durkheim and Max Weber* (London: Cambridge University Press, 1971), 171–172.
14. Weber, *Prophets*, 37.
15. Weber *Prophets*, 37.
16. Weber *Prophets*, 37–38.
17. Thomas O'Dea, who develops Weber's thesis, provides a brief account of the journey of Christianity from the life of Jesus the Prophet to the institutionalised Church in *The Sociology of Religion* (Englewood Cliffs, New Jersey: Prentice Hall, 1963), 37–51.

For our purposes it is sufficient to note that Christianity began with a 'charismatic' leader, and that the movement has since undergone a process of 'routinisation'. That is to say, the church has evolved from a spontaneous creative community based around the qualities of an individual personality; to a stable community with set patterns of worship, beliefs and organisational structures.[18]

Our concern is that, given the church is now institutionalised, what problems will this create? And if those problems include being irrelevant to youth, what then is the solution? Let us now turn our attention to the challenges that face the institutionalised church.

Thomas O'Dea: Institutional dilemmas

O'Dea, developing and systematising the work of Weber, offers for us the clearest analysis of the challenges that face systems that have undergone a process of 'routinisation'. Therefore we shall use his work as a framework for critiquing the modern church. He postulates that there are five dilemmas that will face the institutionalised church.[19]

First, the dilemma of mixed motivation. The original zeal and 'single-mindedness' of the movement is replaced by the personal agendas of subsequent leaders. Thus O'Dea says:

> Institutionalization brings about a situation in which religious practitioners, especially those who occupy official statuses, are placed in a position where not only devotion to the ideas of the religious organization but also self interest in terms of prestige and career are mobilized behind the prescribed behavior.[20]

Second, the dilemma of administrative order. Basically put, this means an elaborate bureaucracy versus an effective structure. Not only can an organisation grow to an unmanageable size, but it can also be ill-equipped to cope with new challenges. In the context of the local church, this often leaves the senior minister balancing the demands of the dated bureaucracy and his local church.

Third, the dilemma of power. As a religion grows it is in danger of becoming more like the popular culture. There is a 'subtle temptation for religious leaders to avail themselves of close relation between

---

18. O'Dea, 37–38.
19. T. O'Dea, 'Five Dilemmas of the Institutionalization of Religion'. *Journal for the Scientific Study of Religion* 1 No 1 (Oct), 30–41.
20. O'Dea, *The Sociology of Religion*, 77.

religion and general cultural values in order to reinforce the position of religion itself'.[21]

Fourth, the dilemma of delimitation. O'Dea identifies two potential dangers in the transmission of the charismatic moment into words that address everyday situations. On the one hand, there is the danger for the original message to be watered down so as to be socially more acceptable. On the other hand, there is the danger of the letter of the law being applied legalistically, and killing the spirit and its initiating spark.

Fifth, the dilemma of the Symbolic. In the process of translating the charismatic moment into ritual, and attaching symbols to that ritual, the unexpected becomes represented in the expected. It thus fails to elicit any response, robbing the ritual of any meaning.

It is my contention that the church's reaction to each of these five dilemmas serves to alienate the institutionalised church from postmodern Australian youth. As regards the dilemma of mixed motivation, youth have a general apathy towards the office of 'priest'. People in modern societies are not respected on the basis of their position, but rather on the basis of their personality or their gifts.[22] Australians in fact tend to distrust authority figures. If priests are suspected of having their own interests at heart, then they are held in the same esteem as politicians – whom Australians regard with great cynicism.[23]

As regards the dilemma of administrative order, there is again a general perception of bureaucracies as inefficient, unreliable, and impersonal. Accessing welfare services from church agencies can feel like applying for unemployment benefits from a government department. Given that youth have been raised in a highly individualistic culture, they despise being treated as a number.

Likewise, Australians have always had a dislike of those in positions of authority. Given our convict roots we have always barracked for the underdog and the outlaw. From the beginning 'the Established Church

---

21. O'Dea as cited by M. Poloma, *The Assemblies of God at the Crossroads: Charisma and Institutional Dilemmas* (Knoxville: University of Tennessee Press, 1989), 96–97.
22. Note that Hugh Mackay identifies this process occurring in Australian politics in *Reinventing Australia: The Mind and Mood of Australia in the 90's* (Sydney: Angus and Robertson, 1993), 171–174.
23. Mackay, 169–191.

was closely identified with the State and the *status quo*, its clerical representatives were all too often linked with any injustice or abuse of the system.'[24] In the process of marrying itself to that ethos and era, the church has divorced itself from subsequent generations. Conversely, adolescents have always defined themselves against the values of their primary socialisation (that is, their parents), and are prone to challenging the authority of the status quo.[25]

The dilemma of delimitation can be clearly seen outworking itself in the 'liberal' movements that affect all mainstream churches, but perhaps most consistently the Uniting Church. In Liberalism the message is 'watered down' and flavoured with popular values. The church then becomes very much like a social action group and has nothing unique or substantial to offer young people.[26]

The dilemma of the Symbolic is equally a problem, as is most clearly seen in High Anglicanism. As the 'unexpected' is repeatedly represented with the expected, it fails to elicit an emotional response. Icons are emptied of their intrinsic meaning, and what is left is only the transient meaning attributed by the observer. People do not 'feel' that they have come into contact with the 'holy'.[27] For postmodern youth, where truth is more about feeling than logic or tradition, this will not constitute a satisfactory service.[28]

Anglican Primate of Australia, Dr Keith Rayner, sums up the above problems when he says 'We have to confess that the Church does not have the credibility with youth that it should ... There is a cultural gap we have not effectively bridged.[29] In most mainstream churches, people aged 15 to 30 are significantly under-represented.[30] Thus it appears that O'Dea's prediction that institutional dilemmas would make the church an increasingly irrelevant institution to youth are being realised in the marketplace.

---

24. A.M. Grocott, *Convicts, Clergyman and Churches: Attitudes of Convicts and Ex-Convicts Towards the Churches and Clergy in New South Wales from 1788 to 1851* (Sydney: Sydney University Press, 1980), 280–284.
25. I. Robertson, *Sociology* (New York: Worth, 1982), 123–124.
26. Note that the Uniting Church has the worst Young Adult Retention rate. P. Kaldor et al, *Shaping A Future* (Adelaide: Open Book, 1997), 27.
27. Bocock as cited by Gill, 374.
28. The Anglican Church has the second worst young adult retention rate. Kaldor, 27.
29. Rayner as quoted in *The Australian*, see appendix 1.
30. NCLS as cited by *The Australian*, see appendix 1.

The knee jerk reaction at this point would be think that what is needed is a solution to the dilemmas that institutionalisation brings. Yet this would be to misunderstand O'Dea. The dilemmas are not so much problems to solve and make go away as they are inevitable tensions that will constantly need to be managed.[31] In fact, to lock a church into today's solution is to commit yourself to greater institutionalisation and irrelevance tomorrow.

The charismatic leader as Weber's solution

Before reviewing Weber's solution let us briefly review the problem at hand, with specific reference to Weber's analysis of power. We have an institutionalised church that struggles for relevancy with postmodern Australian youth, and the current (irrelevant) practices are legitimised by either rational or traditional sources of power.

Traditional authority gains its warrant from the 'sanctity of age-old rules and powers'.[32] That is to say we do things this way and we value these offices in our institution because we always have.

Rational or legal authority on the other hand, lies within an elaborate system of rules and regulations defining rights and obligations. People hold the power to do the things they do not because of who they are, or the traditional esteem with which their office is held, but because of the defined authority and responsibility that is attached to their position. There is no authority other than that which the system ordains.[33]

Note that Weber's process of 'routinisation' involves a movement away from the 'charismatic' moment and leader, and toward traditional and rational-legal authority. Note also that the dilemmas of institutionalisation, as identified by O'Dea, are dilemmas that are inherent to traditional and rational-legal systems. Thus it comes as no surprise that Weber's solution to the above-mentioned dilemmas will not come from either the traditional or the rational systems; for they are part of the problem. Rather the solution will be found in the form of a new 'charismatic' leader.

Weber defines charisma as 'a certain quality of an individual personality

---

31. Systems Management is an approach to church management built on managing and not solving tension. The definitive text in this discipline is E.H. Friedman, *Generation to Generation: Family Process in Church and Synagogue* (Guildford Press, 1985).
32. Weber as cited by Giddens, 156.
33. Giddens, 157–158.

by virtue of which he is considered extraordinary and treated as endowed with supernatural, superhuman, or at least specifically exceptional powers or qualities'.[34] Whether or not this is in fact true is irrelevant. The point is that he is attributed these qualities. The appropriate response to such a leader is to zealously follow.[35]

Gathering around him those who follow his leadership rather than the traditional or legal rules, the charismatic leader can then be an agent of change. Gill sees 'Charisma [as] a driving, creative force which surges through the established rules, whether traditional or legal, which govern an existing order'.[36] Simply speaking, the charismatic leader can use his charisma to introduce a new period of dynamism into the social processes. The traditional irrelevant structures can be replaced with newer more relevant ones.[37]

The charismatic leader and the Trinitarian community

While Weber himself was not interested in the 'fit' that exists between the charismatic leader and the Trinitarian community, we shall now make that our focus. Trinitarian theology rightly understood is not an abstract doctrine, but a foundational set of principles for thinking about the life and shape of the church.[38] For Gunton 'the Church is what it is by virtue of being called to be a temporal echo of what it is that the eternal community of God is'.[39]

Migliore outlines three 'interpretive statements' about God as Trinity. First, *'the eternal life of God is personal life in relationship'*.[40] God cannot be defined statically, or only by reference to his attributes. His dynamic relationships are at the core of who he is. Second, *'God exists in community'*.[41] God is essentially communal in his dealings with himself

---

34. Weber, *Economy and Society*, vol 1, 241.
35. Gill, 160–161.
36. Giddens, 161.
37. Spector and Kitsuse as cited by Robertson, 587, have seen this process of charismatic moments giving birth to new social movements; those movements receiving public legitimisation and then becoming bogged down by bureaucracy; leading to a re-emergence of the original zeal as a life cycle that typifies many social movements.
38. C.E. Gunton, *The Promise of a Trinitarian Theology* (Edinburgh: T&T Clark, 1997), 56–57.
39. Gunton, 78.
40. D.L. Migliore, *Faith Seeking Understanding: An Introduction to Christian Theology* (Grand Rapids: Eerdmans, 1991), 67. Emphasis his.
41. Migliore, 69. Emphasis his.

and his creation. Third, *'the life of God is essentially self-giving love'*.[42] Not only within the Godhead, but especially in his dealings with the fallen world, God continuously demonstrates himself to be loving and gracious.

If the church's ontology is derived from that of God, and if its life is to echo that of the Trinitarian community, then there will be several inherent tensions between the institutionalised church and the charismatic leader who is seeking to reignite the dynamic processes of his or her church.

First there is the tension in what it means for a leader to have 'charisma'. Central to Weber's definition is that it is a personality trait that belongs to the individual. Given that it is necessary for the charismatic leader to gather followers in order to ensure the long term survival of his/her movement – can this not be understood as forming a faction? And is this not then a faction formed around an individual?

This has raised fears in many people's minds. All too often I have heard anecdotal stories of youth workers who have gathered around them many youth; but when the leader leaves the local church - the youth disappear too. This phenomenon sounds not unlike that which divided the early Corinthian church, where various factions formed around 'charismatic' leaders (1 Corinthians 1:10–17).

A second source of tension will come in that 'charismatic' leaders define themselves and what they stand for in opposition to the current yet dated practices of the church. In the words of Weber himself: 'The genuine prophet, like the genuine military leader and every true leader in this sense, preaches, creates, or demands *new* obligations'.[43] These new obligations are the outworking of new doctrines. How can leaders at one level be attacking an institution that at another level they themselves are necessarily a part of?

Where does this leave our charismatic leader, the church and change?

Some people will contend that on the basis of this analysis there is no room for individual bearers of 'charisma' in leadership of the Christian community. Such people will tend to see the ideal youth leader as

---

42. Migliore, 70. Emphasis his.
43. Weber, *Economy and Society,* vol 1, 243.

something like a bland arrow: someone who has nothing attractive within him or herself, but rather one who points others to Christ. It is my contention that if we agree with such conclusions we sell ourselves short, and fail to capitalise on the 'agents of change' that bearers of charisma can be in our institutionalised and at times irrelevant church. However, more needs to be said, and some qualifiers need to be placed on the role of such a person.

Let us address the first criticism. Namely, do 'charismatic' leaders necessarily gather people around **themselves** as opposed to Christ? Clearly this understanding is too simplistic. While such leaders do attract a following as a result of their personality, for Weber charisma can be used to challenge an existing order. The goal of the Christian charismatic leader ought not to be to gain a following, but to effect change.

Is this not the pattern we see with Paul himself? Paul is identified in 1 Corinthians as one of the leaders around whom there had gathered a following (1 Corinthians 1:12). Yet he does not tell people to stop following him. On the contrary, he says 'Be imitators of me, as I am of Christ' (1 Corinthians 11:1). In other words, Paul is trying to use whatever following he has to change the existing and often ungodly order at Corinth, so that people might be more like Christ.

Let us turn our attention to the second criticism: that charismatic leaders necessarily define themselves in opposition to existing order, so how then can they be a part of that order? Again this understanding is too simplistic. First it represents in part a misunderstanding of Weber. It is built on the premise that all bureaucracies are evil things. That they are slow and inefficient producers bogged down by 'red tape'. In this view, from time to time all bureaucracies actually need a charismatic leader to come and to change them, lest they become so irrelevant that they peter out and die.

Yet this is not Weber's understanding of a bureaucracy. Weber saw bureaucracies as 'indispensable', and as a most efficient vehicle for the processing of information and the administration that a mass market demands.[44] Granted there may be exceptions to the rule, but it is the

---

44. Weber as cited by Giddens, 159–160.

'calculability' of a rational-legal authority system that predisposes it to a bureaucratic administration.[45]

Within Weber's thesis, the most fertile environment for producing a 'charismatic leader' is an inefficient system. This will be a system against which one can define oneself, and in which one is more likely to gain a following. To translate this back to the question of the institutionalised church, it is when the church is irrelevant and outdated that the charismatic leader is most likely to succeed in gathering a following and challenging the existing order.[46]

Is it not too shallow to simply point the finger at the protagonist when the whole system is in need of change? Rather Paul's analysis of the body of Christ appears to do more justice to the reality of the situation (1 Corinthians 12:12–31). That is to say that the charismatic leader is acting something like the 'infection control system' of the body, which kicks in when things are not as they should be. In this framework, the charismatic leader is understood to be a key part of the Trinitarian community, and not someone who stands in opposition to it.

As regards the 'new obligations' resulting from new doctrines; again these can often be most adequately explained not as imported doctrines foreign to Christianity, but as a refocusing on lost central truths. Allow me to illustrate. Joseph Smith used his charisma to introduce foreign doctrines, and in the process distort Christianity into Mormonism. This is obviously illegitimate. Philip Jensen uses his charisma to refocus people on the central role the Word of God plays in the life of his people. Such an outcome is not only legitimate, but one could argue desirable and necessary to the continued life and growth of the church.[47]

---

45. Weber as cited by Giddens, 160.
46. Is this not the context of the Reformation? Note here that this is a potential weak point in Weber's thesis. J.C. Collins and J.I. Porras in *Built to Last* (New York: Harper Business, 1997) would contend that efficient bureaucracies can engender a culture of raising up 'charismatic' leadership from within. There is no need for a crisis as a catalyst in this process.
47. Another way in which new obligations can be demanded of disciples is by denying ownership of existing doctrines to other groups. Thus the Pentecostal movement may say of the mainstream churches that they do not have the 'real' Spirit, or his 'full' blessing. Theologically speaking the issue then becomes how much weight ought particular doctrines be given, and how will this weighting be reflected in the attention given to other doctrines, and in the life of the church.

Conclusion

Allow me to break with academic tradition at this point, and tailor my conclusions to an audience of those who minister to youth; to an audience who may often feel the frustration of being part of an established institution that is at times irrelevant to youth; to an audience who are often being given the task of somehow solving this problem, yet who are required to do so by playing within the existing rules.

First, let me clarify what I am not saying. I am not necessarily endorsing the perspective that the only solution will come in the form of a 'charismatic leader'. Even Weber himself does not propose this to be the case. What I am saying is that the 'charismatic leader' is one option, and given Weber's insights a likely option.

For any aspiring 'charismatic leaders' let me offer the following advice. By all means use your charismatic charm, but keep the goal as effecting change and not gathering people around yourself.

Second, gather around yourself a group of followers, but let them follow you as you follow Christ. Remember that Christ is always the head of his church, and your task is integrate young people into his body. Your task is not to displace Christ and lead a renegade faction.

Third, take seriously your role as an interpreter of meaning and an attributer of worth. If you are seeking to change anything, make sure that the 'new obligations' and 'new doctrines' you are pushing are not new at all. Make sure they are at least 2,000 years old, and borrowed from someone far wiser than yourself. Remember that there may be gaps in your thinking just as there are in the thinking of others.

Remember also that you are not thinking in a vacuum. Rather you are thinking in a community where others are also thinking and feeling. The task at hand is not so much to solve the dilemmas, but to manage the tensions they create. These tensions can only be managed in the context of a Christian community where all are considerate of the needs of others, including those currently outside the community.

Finally love your church. In fact I can offer no better summary than Jesus himself. Love God and love others as yourself.